T0021576

PhD

Other books by Jorge Cham:

"Piled Higher and Deeper: A Graduate Student Comic Strip Collection"

"Life is Tough and then You Graduate: The Second Piled Higher and Deeper Comic Strip Collection"

Scooped!

The Third *Piled Higher & Deeper* Comic Strip Collection

by

Jorge Cham

Piled Higher and Deeper Publishing
Los Angeles, California

Published by Piled Higher & Deeper, LLC
Los Angeles, California

www.phdcomics.com

Third Printing, February 2012
PRINTED IN CANADA

ISBN-10: 0-9721695-3-9
ISBN-13: 978-0-9721695-3-0

Library of Congress Control Number: 2007902192

U. Libre de Bruxelles, Aalborg U., Denmark, Aarhus U., Abo Akademi U., Academia Sinica, Taiwan, Adelaide U. adelphi U., admu, AdMU, Philippines, Ajou U., albany, Albert Einstein College of Medicine, Albert-Ludwig U. Freiburg, Alicante, Spain, Alliant Int Univ, Alliant International U., Alphatech, Inc., ALU Freiburg, American Business School Paris, American InterContinental U., American U., American U., american U., washington dc, AmericanMilitaryU., Amsterdam, Anna U., India, Appalachian State, APTS, Argosy U.-Chicago NW, Aristotle U. of Thessaloniki, Arizona State U., Arkansas State, ASB denmark, Asia English School, Asian Institute of Technology - Thailand, ateneo de manila U., Athens U. of Economics and Business, AUBG, auburn U., Auckland Uni, Austin Peay State U., Australian National U., Canberra, avignon U., france, Azusa Pacific U., B M S C E, Baker College, Baldwin-Wallace College, Ball State, Ball State U., Balliol College, Oxford U., Baltic Business School, Kalmar, Sweden, Baltic State Technical U., St.Petersburg,, bangalore U., Bangor U., UK, Barrackpur Government High School, India, barry U., baruch, bastyr.edu, Bauhaus U. Weimar (Germany), Baylor, Beijing U. of Posts &Telecomm, Bellarmine U., belmont, Belmont U., Benedictine U., Ben-Gurion U. in the Negev, Israel, Bharatidasan Univ, India, Bilgi U., Turkey, bilkent U., Binghamton U., Birkbeck College (UK), Birmingham U., BITS, Pilani, Black Hills State U., Blekinge Institute of Technology, Bloomsburg U., BMSCE, Bangalore, Bogazici U. Turkey, Boise State Univ, bologna, Boston College, Boston U., Boun, Bournemouth U., Bowdoin College, Bowling Green State U., Brandeis U., Brazilian Space Research Institute, BRICS, Bridgewater State College, Brigham Young U., Brock U., Brookes U.-UK, Brookhaven, Brooks College, Brown U., Brunel U., Bryant and Stratton, Bryn Mawr, Bryn Mawr College, Bucknell U., Buckwhere, Budapest U. of Technology and Economics, buena terra, Buffalo State College, Business, buyler collage of non medicine, Cal Poly Pomona, Cal State Long Beech, Cal State Sacramento, California College, California Institute of Integral Studies, California Institute of Technology, California State U., Sacramento, Cambridge U., Campbell U., Canley Vale High, Canterbury (NZ), Capella U., Capitol College, Cardiff, cardiff U., Carleton (Ontario, Canada), Carleton (Ottawa, Canada), carleton U., Carnegie Foundation, Carnegie Mellon U., Cascadia CC, Case Western Reserve U., catawba college, Catholic U., cbpf -brazil, CCMb, Hyderabad , India, cea-saclay-France, Cedar Crest College, Cedarville U., Central Michigan U., Central Missouri State U., central queensland U., Central Washington U., centre for water research, Chalmers Technical U., Charles Sturt U., Australia, Charles U., Chicago, chico state, Chinese Culture U., Chinese U. of Hong Kong, Churchill College Cambridge, cibnor, City U. of New York, Brooklyn College, Civil Eng., U. of Tokyo, Claremont Graduate U., Claremont McKenna, Claremont Montessori, Clark U., Clemson U., clermont-ferrand (france), Cleveland State U., CNRS France, Collège de l'Outaouais, College of William & Mary, Colorado College, Colorado School of Mines, Colorado State Universtiy, Columbia U., Commerce, U. of Adelaide, Concordia U., connecticut college, Conservatoire National des Arts et Métiers, Cornell U., Courant Institute, Courtauld Institute of Art, Coventry U., Cranfield U., csiro, australia, CSPP @ Alliant Univ, CSU Bakersfield, CSU Northridge, CSU, Los Angeles, CTH , Sweden, Curtin U. of Technology, cuyahoga community colege (aka Tri-C!), CWRU, Czech Technical U. in Prague, DA-IICT, dakota state U., Dalhousie U., damascus U., Darmstadt Technical U., Dartmouth College, dauphine, Daytona Beach Community College, De La Salle U., Deakin Uni - Australia, Delft U. of Technology, Delhi U., Denbigh High, Departamento de Geociências - JEL, DePaul U., Devry, DLSU-Manila, Dominican U., donga U., douglass college, Drew/FDU, Drexel U., Dublin City U., Duke U., Duquesne U., Durham U., D'Youville College, EAESP-FGV, east carolina U., East Stroudsburg U., East TN State U., Eastern Illinois U., Eastern Kentucky U., eastern mediterranean U., Eastern Michigan U., Eastman School of Music, Ecole Centrale, Ecole Centrale de Nantes (France), Ecole Centrale Lyon, Ecole Centrale Paris, Ecole des Mines de Nantes (France), Ecole des Mines de Saint-Etienne, Ecole Normale Superieure, Ecole Polytechnique de Tours, École Polytechnique Fédérale de Lausanne, Ecole Polytechnique, Paris, Ecoles des Mines de Nantes, ECP (France), ECU, Edgewod High School, Edgewood, Edinburgh U., UK, EGS, eindhoven U. of technology, eivd - Switzerland, Elizabethtown College, Emanuel Luthren, EMBL, Emerson College, Emmanuel School of Religion, Emn (France), Emory U., Emporia State U. EMU, ENIM (FRANCE), ENS (Paris) (France), ENS Cachan (France), ENS Lyon (France) | INRIA Sophia Antipolis (France), ENSEEIHT,France, ENSIMAG, ENSM Douai, EPFL - Lausanne, EPFL, Switzerland, EPGE - FGV / RJ - Brazil, EPHE (france), Erasmus University, Rotterdam, the Netherlands, ERAU, ESB-UCP, ESC Grenoble, France, Escola Paulista de Medicina - Brazil, Escola Politécnica - USP - Brazil, ETH zurich, switzerland, Ewha Womans U., ewha(in RoK), EWU, Exeter, faculty of arts Ljubljana, Faithway Baptist College, Fashion Institute of Technology, FAST-NU, FCM-UABC, FCT, FCUL (in Portugal) Federal U. of Minas Gerais, Brazil, Federal U. of Rio de Janeiro, Federal U. of Rio Grande do Sul, Brazil, Federal U. of Santa Catarina - Brazil, Federal U. of São Carlos - Brazil, Fermilab / Nikhef, FEUP, FFCA, FGV-EAESP, FGV-EAESP, Brazil, Fielding Graduate Institute, FIU, Fletcher School of Law and Diplomacy, Flinders U. of South Australia, Florida A&M U., Florida Atlantic U., florida gulf coast univrsity, Florida Institute of Tech, Florida International U., Florida State U., FNAL, Foothill College, Fordham, Framingham State College, Fraunhofer IPSI, Free U. Amsterdam, Freie Universitaet, Berlin, fribourg Univ, CH, fritz-haber-institaet, FSU, FU berlin, Fundacao Getulio Vargas, Fuqua School of Business, Duke U., Gakushuin, Galway, Ireland, Gannon U., Erie, PA, GATE, France, Geneva College, Gent, Belgium, george fox U., George Mason U., George Washington U., Georgetown U., georgia institute of technology, Georgia State U., Georgia Tech, GES, Gettysburg College, GGSB, GIIS, Geneva (Switzerland), glasgow U., Glasgow, Scotland, gmu, Goa Institute of MaNAGEMENT, Göteborg U. Sweden, Gothenburg U., Gradurate Institute of International Studies, Geneva U., Switzerland, Granada (Spain), Grand Valley State U., Grenoble - France, Griffith U., Grinnell College, Grove City College, gsu, Guelph U., Gulbenkian, gvsu, GWU, H U., h&s, Hamilton College, Hanyang U. Korea, Harvard Divinity School, Harvard Extension School, Harvard Law School, Harvard Medical School, Harvard U., Harvey Mudd, HAU, Haverford College, HCC, HCU, Hebrew U., HEC, HEC Montreal, HEC Paris, Heidelberg U., Helsinki U. of Technology, Heriot watt U., Edinburgh, UK, Heriot Watt, Scotland Hesser college, Hill Grange, HK Polytechnic Univ, HKU, HKUST, Hofstra U., Högskolan i Skövde, Hokkaido U., JAPAN, Hong Kong Polytechnic U., Hong Kong U., Hong Kong U. of Science and Technology, Howard U., HRI,India, HU, HUJ, Hull U., UK, Humboldt U., Hunter college, HUT, HVC, HY, I.I.Sc, bangalore, india, I.I.T Delhi, I.I.T Kanpur, I.S of Cape Town South Africa, IAS, ia-unam, IC, ICR London, Idaho State U., idiap research institute, switzerland, IFSIC, IGIDR, IIIT, iiita, iiitb, IIIT-Hyd, India, IIIT-Hyderabad, IIM B, IIM Bangalore, IISc Bangalore, India, IIT - Delhi, IIT Bomaby, IIT Kanpur, India, IIT Kharagpur, India, IIT Madras, IIT Madras,India, iit roorkee, IIT, Chicago, Illinois Institute Of Technology, Illinois School of Professional Psychology, Illinois State U., Illinois Wesleyan, Imperial College London, IMSc,Chennai, INA P-G, France, Indiana State U., Indiana U., Industrial Light + Magic, INECOL, INP Toulouse, inpg, INPG (France), inria, INRS-Eau, terre et Environnement, Insa, INSA de Lyon (France), INSA de Rouen - France, Insead, France, InSIA, Paris (France) http://www.insia.org, Institute of International Studies, Geneva, Instituto Balseiro, Instituto Superior Técnico, International Graduate School for genetics and Functional Genomics, Cologne, International Institute of Information Technology, Bangalore, Iowa State U., IPH, IPI PAN, Poland, IPICYT, Iran's national U., IRISA Rennes France, IRISA/INRIA, IRMA, ISEG, IST, IST - Lisbon, Portugal, Istanbul Technical U., ISU, IT U. of Copenhagen, ITB Indonesia, ITEE, U. of Queensland, ITESM (Monterrey, Mexico), ITESM, Cuernavaca, MX, ITM, ITS, itu, IU, iucaa, IUCAA India, IUCAA, Pune, IUE, IUHEI Geneva, IUP, IUPUI, Jacksonville U., James Cook U., Queensland, Australia, JCB, UofT, JMDC, jncasr, JNV, Jodrell Bank Observatory, John Jay College of Criminal Justice, Johns Hopkins U., JPSM, JU, Jussieu - Paris - France, Justus-Liebig-Universität, Giessen, Germany, K.U.Leuven, Belgium, KAIST, Korea, kansas city U. of medicine and biosciences, Kansas State U., Kapteyn Institute, U. of Groningen, Karlsruhe TH, Karolinska Institutet, Katholieke U.it Leuven, Katholieke U.it Nijmegen, KDI School of Public Policy and Managment, keele U., Keio U., Japan, Keller Graduate School Management - Chicago Il, kellogg, Kenan-Flagler Business School, Kennedy School of Gov't, Kennesaw State U., Kent at Canterbury, Kent State, Kettering U., KGSM, Kiel-Germany, King Ludwig-Maximilians U. in Munich, Bava, King's College London, Kingston, KMV, Delhi U., KNT, KNToosi, KNTU, Kobe U., Koc U., kongy engineering college, KTH, Sweden, KU, KU Leuven, KU Med Center, Kyoto U., Kyung Hee U., Kyungpook National U., La Plata, Argentina, La Sapienza - Rome, La Sierra U., La Trobe Uni, Melbourne,Australia, LAAS-CNRS, France, Lady Margaret Hall, Oxford, Lakehead U., Lancaster U., UK, LaSalle, Latrobe U., Laval U., LBS, lcg-unam, Leeds Uni, Lehigh U., Lehman College, Leiden U., life (Canty, Alberta), Linfield College, Linköping U., Sweden, LNEC, Loma Linda U., London Business School, Long Island U., New York, Loughborough U., UK, Louisiana State U., Louisiana Tech U., Loyola College in Maryland, Loyola Marymount, Loyola U. Chicago, LTH, LTU, Luleå U. of Technology, LUMS, Lund U., Lycee Le Castel, Lycoming College, M.E.S.C.O.E, Maastricht U. (Netherlands), macalester, Macquarie U., Madonna U., madras school of economics, Madrid U., Spain, MAHE, Malaspina U., malrau, Manchester U., Mannheim, Germany, marquette uni., Marcuette U., Marshall U., Masaryk U. Brno, Czech Republic, massachusetts college of pharmacy, Massachusetts Institute of Technology, max planck institute for human development, germany, Max-Planck-Insitute for Solid State Research (Germany), Mayo Graduate School, Mays Business School, McCormick Theological Seminary, McGill University, McMaster U., Medical College of Virginia, Medical College of Wisconsin, Medical U. of South Carolina, Medical U. Vienna, Austria, Melbourne U., Memorial U. of Newfoundland, Mepco, Mesa State, METU/Turkey, Miami U., Miami U., Ohio, Miami-Dade College, Michigan St Univ, Michigan State U., Michigan Technological U., Michigan-Ann Arbor, middle east technical U., Middle Tennessee State U., USA, Middle TN State U., Midwestern U., Mighigan State U., Milton Hershey School, Milwaukee School of Engineering, Mississippi State U., MLU Halle-Wittenberg, MMU, MNSU, Mankato, Monash U., Australia, Montana State U., Monterrey Tech (México), Montgomery College, Montreal Polytechnic, Morehead State U., Morelia Inst. Tech., Moscow State Institute of Electronics and Mathemat, Moscow State U., Mount Holyoke College, Mount Sinai School of Medicine, Mt. San Anto[...]pier, Nat. U. Singapore, National Centre for Biological Sciences, Bangalore, National Cheng Kung U., National Chiao Tung U., National Institute of Fashion Technology, National Sun Yat-sen U., Taiwan, National Taiwan U., Nationa[...]of Singapore, National Yang-Ming U. in Taiwan, Naval Postgraduate School, NBRC, NCBS, India, NCKU, NCSU, NCTU,Taiwan, NDSU, New College of Florida, new mexico state U., New Mexico Tech, New School for Social Resea[...]IOO, NIP, NIST, NIT Calicut India, NJIT, NLH, NMIMS, NMSU, North Carolina A & T State Uinversity, North Carolina Central U., North Carolina State U., North Dakota State U., North Texas, Northeastern U., Northern Arizona U., Northern Illinois U., Northwest Missouri State U., Northwestern U., Norwegian U. Sci. & Tech., Notre Dame, Notre Dame U. Australia, Nottingham U., Nova, Nova High, Nova Southeastern U., NTNU, NTU, NTUA Athens Greece, NUI Galway, Ireland, NUI Maynooth, Ireland, NUS, nust, zimbabwe, NWU, NYIT, NYPD Dog school, Oakland U., Oberlin, Observatoire de Paris, Occidental College, Ohio State U., Ohio U., OISE/UT, Oklahoma Christian U., Oklahoma State U./Auburn U., Oklahoma State U.---Stillwater, Olathe Northwest High School, Old Dominion U., ONWA Amsterdam, Open U., UK, Oregon Graduate Institute, Oregon Health & Science U. Oregon State U., orsay U., OSSU, Oswego State U., Otago U., New Zealand, Our Lady of the Lake U., Oxford Brookes U., Oxford U., UK, ozark tech college, Pace, Pacific U., Palermo, PASADENA CITY COLLEGE, Paul Sabatier U., Peking U., Penn State U., Pepperdine, Perkins Seminary - SMU, PESIT, PGSP, Philipps-U. of Marburg, Phoenix U., Pioneer Junior College, PISIS, Pittsburgh, PKU, PLU, PNU. KOREA, Pohang U. of Science and Technology, Point Park U., Poitiers' U., polaris, Politecnico di Milano, Poly, Polytechnic School of the U. of Sao Paulo, Pontificia U. CAtolica del Peru, Portland State U., Porto, POSTECH, Korea, princeton U., Provence U., PSG College of Technology, PUC. Chile, PUCMM, Purdue U., pure maths U. of Adelaide, Queen Mary, U. of London, Queens College - CUNY, Queens U. Belfast, Queen's U., Kingston, QUT, R.C.S.I., Radford U., Reading U., Rechester., reed college, Regensburg, Rennes, Rensselaer Polytechnic Institute, rhode island college, Rhodes College, Rhodes U., Grahamstown , south Africa, Rice U., RIJKSU.IT GRONINGEN, THE NETHERLANDS, Rio Grande do Sul Federal U., Brazil, RIT, RMC, RMIT U., Rochester Institute of Technology, Rockefeller U., Roehampton U., Rose-Hulman Institute, Rowan, Royal College Of Port Louis (Mauritius), Royal Holloway, U. of London, RuG (Netherlands), Russell Sage College, Rutgers U., Rutgers, Fermilab, Rutherford Appleton Lab, RWTH-AAchen, Ryerson, S.d.College, S.D.S.U., S.N.U, Saarbruecken U., Germany, Saarland U., Germany, Sabanci University Istanbul, Sacred Hearts, Saint Anselm College, Saint Joseph's U., Saint Louis U., Saint Mary's U., Saint Michael's College, SAIT, Sam Houston State U., San Diego State U., San Francisco State U., San Jose State U., Santa Clara U., santa fe community college, SCE, NTU, Singapore, Sciences Po Paris, Scripps College, Scripps Inst. of Oceanography, Scripps research institute, SCSU, SCU, SDSU, SDSU/UCSD, SDU, Denmark, Seattle U., Seoul National U., SESS Kranj, Seton Hall U, Seton Hall U., SFU, SGGS, ShanDong Univ, Sharjah College, sheffield U., Sherbrooke U., Shippensburg U., Shiraz U., shorter college, SIG Simmons College, Simon Fraser U., simon's rock college, SIO, SIU, SIUC, SIUE, SLIET, SLU, Sweden, SMI, Curtin U., Smith College, SMU, SNU, korea, Sogang U., Sorbonne U., Southampton U., Southeast Missouri State U., Southern Christian U., Southern Illinois U., Southern Illinois U. Carbondale, Southern Methodist U., Southern Nazarene U., southern polytechnic, Southern U., Southwest Missouri State U., Southwest TX State U. Springfield College, SPRU - U. of Sussex, SSE Helsinki, sssihl, St Andrews, St John's College, Cambridge, St Peter's, St. Louis U., St. Mary's College of MD, St. Olaf College, St.Josephs, st.marys academy St.Thomas U., Stanford U., Stella Maris, Stellenbosch U., Stern Business School, NYU, Stevens Institute of Technology, Stockholm U., STONY BROCK U., Strathclyde Uni, Strayer U., Stuttgart U., Sundland Uni UK, Sungkyunkwan U. in R.O.K, SUNY Albany, SUNY at Stony Brook, SUNY Binghamton, SUNY Buffalo, SUNY SB, SUNY Stony Brook, Surrey U., Swarthmore, Swedish School of Economics & BA, Helsinki, Swiss Federal Institute of Technology, Lausanne, Sydney U., Syracuse U., SZABIST, Tampere technical U., Tampere U. of Technology, Tanaka Business School, Imperial College London, Tartu U., Estonia, Tata Institute, TCD, Dublin, teachers college, Teaneck High School, Tec Morelia, Tech, Tech U.Vienna, Austria, Technical Research & Development Institute, Technical U, Berlin, Technical U. of Catalonia, Technical U. of Lisbon, Technical U. of Munich, Department of Life, Technion - Israel, Technion, Israel, Technische Universitaet Muenchen, Technische Universität Graz, tel aviv U., Telecom Paris, Temple U., Tennesee, Tennessee Technological U., texas A & M U., Texas A&M U.-Kingsville, texas christian U., Texas State U., Texas Tech U., the American U. in Cairo (Ga Tech Alum), The Catholic U. of America, the Chinese U. of Hong Kong, The Citadel, The College of New Jersey, The Evergreen State College, The George Washington U., The Hong Kong Polytechnic U., The Rockefeller U., The U. of Georgia, The U. of Hong Kong, The U. of Melbourne, Australia, The U. of Michigan, The U. of Pennsylvania, The U. of Queensland, The U. of Scranton, The U. of Southern Mississippi, The U. of Texas @ Austin, The U. of Texas at Austin, The U. of Western Ontario, the U. of york, The Walter and Eliza Hall Institute of Mecical Res, The Wharton School - U. of PA, Theological Union, TIFR, Timpview, ToDai, Tohoku, Japan, Tokyo Institute of Tech., Tokyo U. Graduate School, toledo, Towson U., Trent U., Trier U., Germany, Trinity College, Cambridge, UK, Trinity College, Dublin, Ireland, Trinity U., troy state U., Tsinghua U., TU Darmstadt - Germany, TU Delft, TU Graz, Austria, TU Munich, Germany, TU of Varna, TU Vienna, TU Wien, Austria, Tufts U., Tulane U., U. Akron, U. Alberta, U. Arizona, U. AZ, U. Buenos Aires, U. C. Berkeley, U. Cal. Berkeley, U. Chicago, U. Colorado/Boulder, U. Connecticut, U. Dayton, U. Laval (Quebec, Canada), U. Maryland, U. Mass. Lowell, U. Michigan, U. Minnesota, U. Montana, U. Notre Dame, U. of Akron, U. of Alaska Fairbanks, U. of Arizona, U. of Calgary, U. of Chicago, U. of Colorado, U. of Colordao at Boulder, U. of Grenoble - France, u. of guelph, U. of Illinois, U. of Illinois Urbana-Champaign, U. of Kansas, U. of Kentucky, U. of Maryland, U. of Michigan, U. of Montana, U. of North Texas, U. of Pennsylvania, U. of Pittsburgh, U. of Rochester, U. of Saskatchewan, U. of Sydney, U. of Tokyo, U. of Virginia, U. of Washington, U. of Windsor, U. Penn., U. Pittsburgh, U. Pompeu Fabra, U. Texas, Austin, U. Utah, U. Washington, U. Wisconsin, Madison, U.C. Irvine, U.C. Riverside, U.C.Berkeley, U.Mich, UFR besancon, france, ufr ima (france), UFRGS -Brazil, UFSC, Brazil, UH Manoa, UiB, Norway, ULA, Venezuela, ULB (Brussels), UMass Amherst, UMass Boston, Umass Dartmouth, UMass Lowell, Umass Med, Umeå U., Sweden, unam, mexico, UNB Fredericton, UNC at Chapel Hill, Uni Augsburg (germany), uni of queensland (australia), Uni of Reading, Uni of Sydney, uni of tasmania, australia, Uni of Waikato, Uni of Western Australia, Uni of Wollongong, Uni. of Southampton, UK, Uni. of Wales, Aberystwyth, UNICAMP (Brazil), Uni-Düsseldorf, U. of Westminster - London, U. utrecht, netherlands, Unifersity of Calgary, Uniformed Services U., Union Institute, Union Institute & U., Union Theo Sem, UNISINOS -- Brazil, U.College London, U.of calgary, U.of Cincinnati, U.of colorado, U.of Connecticut, U.of delaware, U.of FL, U.of Florida, U.of georgia, U.of Illinois, U.of Illinois at Urbana-Champaign, U.of Kansas, U.of Kentucky, U.of Maryland, U.of Maryland, College Park, U.of Mass-Amherst, U.of Miami, U.of Michigan, U.of Minn, U.of minnesota, U.of mississippi, U.of Missouri-Rolla, U.of new mexico, U.of North Carolina at Chapel Hill, U.of OKlahoma, U.of Ottawa, U.of Phoenix, U.of Pittsburgh, U.of Rochester, U.of Southampton, U.of Souther California, U.of stockholm, U.of Texas, U.of Texas, Austin, U.of Texas-Austin, U.of toronto, U.of Utah, U.of Washington, U.of Western Ontario, U.of Wisconsin - Madison, U.of Wisconsin Madison, U.Paris 6 - France,, U.savoie, U.So Cal, U.Texas at Dallas, U. "Politehnica" Timisoara, Romania, U. Arizona, U. Cal. San Diego, U. California Santa Barbara, U. Michigan, U. missouri - rolla, U. of aegean, U. of Akron, U. of Arizona, U. of Arkansas U. of art&design helsinki, U. of British Columbia, U. of California - Santa Barbara, U. of Cincinnati, U. of colorado, U. of Colorado, Boulder, U. of Connecticut, U. of Dayton, U. of delaware, U. of Florida, U. of Glasgow, U. of illinois, U. of Illinois at Urbana-Champaign, U. of Illinois, Chicago, U. of iowa, U. of kansas, U. of Maryland, U. of Maryland, College Park, U. of Maryland, U. College, U. of Mass. Amherst, U. of Massachusetts, Amherst, U. of Massachusetts, Lowell, U. of M. U. of Michigan, U. of minn., U. of Minnesota, U. of MO - Rolla, U. of Mumbai, India, U. of New Mexico, U. of North Carolina, U. of Notre Dame, U. Of Patras , Greece, U. of Pennsylvania, U. of Pittsburgh, U. of Sao Paulo, U. of Seville (Spain), U. of South Carolina, U. of South Florida, U. of Southern California, U. of Texas at Austin, U. of Texas at Dallas, U. of Texas Health Sci. Center-San Antonio, U. of Utah, U. of Washington, U. of Waterloo, U. Of Wisconsin-Madison, U. Sevilla, U. Seville, U. Southern Calif., U. Texas- Houston, U. Texas Medical Branch, U. of Auckland, U. of Kent, U. of Kentucky, U. of Arizona, U. of Bath, UK, U. of cambridge, U. of Dundee (both UK), U. of Colorado, U. of Florida, U. of Illinois - Springfield, U. of Illinois, U. of Maryland, U. of Maryland (College Park), U. of Paris X, France, U. of Queensland Australia, U. of Queensland, Australia, U. of Saskatchewan, U. of Texas at Arlington, U. of Texas Austin, U. of Waterloo, U. of Wyoming, Universiy of Cambridge, UK, University of Edinburgh, University of Freiburg, Germany, University of Melbourne, U. Carlos III de Madrid, SPain, U. complutense, spain, U. de Buenos Aires, U. de Murcia, U. del Pacifico (PERU)...hopefully Cornell U. in the near future, U. Iberoamericana, U. Interamericana de Puerto Rico, U. Metropolitana, U. Nacional de Colombia, U. Panamericana, U. Pompeu Fabra, Barcelona, U.e de Coimbra, U.e de Évora, U.e de Lisboa, U.e de São Paulo, U.e de São Paulo, Brazil, U.e do Porto, U.e Federal de Mato Grosso do Sul, U.e Federal do Ceará, U.e Federal do PAraná, Brazil, U.e Regional de Blumenau, Universit of McMaurey, U. of Puerto Rico, Universitat Autonoma de Barcelona, SPAIN, Universität Karlsruhe, U. catholique de Louvain (Belgium), U. de Bourgogne - France, U. de Franche-Comte (France), U. de haute alsace, U. de Lille 1 (France), U. de Moncton, U. de montréal, U. de Nantes, France, U. de Pierre et Marie Curie, U. de Provence (FRANCE), U. de Sherbrooke, U. de Sherbrooke, U. de Toulouse 1 Sciences Sociales, U. Libre de Bruxelles, U. Lille 3, U. Paris, U. Paris 1, U. Paris 6, U. Paris VI, France, U. Paris-Sud, France, U., U. Alabama, U. at Albany, U. at Buffalo, SUNY, U. College Cork, U. College Dublin, U. Cologne, U. Montpellier-France, U. North Carolina Chapel Hill, U. of Aarhus, U. of Aarhus, Denmark, U. of Adelaide, Australia, U. of akron, U. of Ala. / Huntsville, U. of Alabama at Birmingham, U. of Alabama in Huntsville, U. of Alaska Fairbanks, U. of Alaska -Fairbanks, U. of Alberta, U. of Alberta, Canada, U. of amsterdam, U. of antwerp, U. of Antwerp, Belgium, U. of applied science, darmstadt, germany, U. of Arizona, U. of arkansas at little rock, U. of Auckland, U. of Auckland, New Zealand, U. of Aveiro U. Of Ballarat, U. of Barcelona, U. of Barcelona (Spain), U. of Bath, U. Of Bath, England, U. of Bath, UK, U. of Beira Interior, U. of Bergen, U. of Berkeley, California, U. of Birmingham, U. of Birmingham (England), U. of Birmingham, England, U. of Bonn (Ger), U. of Bradford, UK, U. of brighton, uk, U. of bristol, U. of Bristol UK, U. of British Columbia, U. of British Columbia, U. of Buenos Aires, U. of Buffalo, U. of Cagliari Italy, U. of calgary, U. of California, U. of California - Irvine, U. of California at Berkeley, U. of California at Irvine, U. of California at Riverside, U. of California Irvine, U. of California Riverside, U. of california san diego, U. of California San Francisco, U. of California Santa Barbara, U. of California Santa Cruz, U. of California, Berkeley, U. of California, Davis, U. of California, Irvine, U. of california, los angeles, U. of California, Riverside, U. of California, San Diego, U. of California, San Francisco, U. of California, Santa Barbara, U. of California--Berkeley, U. of California-Davis, U. of California-Irvine, U. of Cambridge, U. of Cambridge (Corpus Christi), U. of Cambridge (United Kingdom), U. of Cambridge, UK, U. of Canberra, Australia, U. of canterbury, U. of Canterbury, New Zealand, U. of Canterbury, NZ, U. of cape town, U. of Cape Town, South Africa, U. of Central Arkansas, U. of Central Florida, U. of Chicago, U. of Cincinnati, U. of Coimbra, U. of Coimbra, Portugal - I am an advisor and I want to know all gard students dirty tricks! :), U. of Cologne, U. of computer science, U. of Connecticut Health Center, U. of Copenhagen, Denmark, U. of Crete, Greece, U. of Dayton, U. of Delaware, U. of Denver, U. of Dortmund, Germany, U. of Dundee, U. of Durham, UK, U. of east anglia, U. of Edinburgh, UK, U. of Erlangen-Nuremberg, Germany, U. of Essex UK, U. of Florida, U. of Florida Gainesville, U. of Geneva, U. of geneva, switzerland, U. of Gent, Belgium, U. of Georgia, U. of girona, U. of glamorgan, U. of Glasgow, Scotland, U. of Guelph, U. of Hamburg, Germany, U. of Hawai'i, U. of Hawaii, Manoa, U. of Helsinki, U. of Hertforshire, UK, U. of Hong Kong, U. of Houston, U. of Houston (2yr MA, then applying to any Ph.D program that I can trick into accepting me), U. of Idaho, U. of Illinois, Chicago, U. of Illinois - Springfield, U. of Illinois - Urbana Champaign, U. of Illinois-Chicago, U. of Indonesia, U. of innsbruck (austria), U. of Iowa, U. of Ixford, U. of Joensuu, Dept. of CS, U. of Kaiserslautern, U. of Kansas, U. of Karlsruhe, U. of Kent, U. of Kent at Canterbury, UK, U. of Kentucky, U. of Kiel, U. of Koblenz, U. of Kwazulu-Natal (South Africa), U. of Lausanne, Switzerland, U. of Leeds, U. of Lethbridge, U. of lille france, U. of Limerick, U. of Limerick, Ireland, U. of Linköping, Sweden, U. of Linz, U. of Lisbon, U. of Liverpool, U. of London, U. of Louisiana at Lafayette, U. of Louisiana at Monroe, U. of Maastricht, U. of maastricht, netherlands, U. of Macedonia, U. of Magdeburg, Germany, U. of Maine, U. of Maine, Orono, U. of Mainz, Germany, U. OF MALAYA, U. of Malta, U. of Manchester, U. of Manitoba, U. of Mannheim, Germany, U. of Marburg, U. of Marland, U. of Maryland - College Park, U. of Maryland, Baltimore County, U. of Massachusetts Amherst, U. of Massachusetts Lowell, U. of Massachusetts Medical School, U. of Massachusetts, Amherst, U. of Massachusetts, Hartwick College, U. of Melbourne, Australia, U. of Miami, U. of Michigan, U. of Minnesota, Duluth, U. of minnesota--twin cities, U. of Mississippi, U. of Missouri - Columbia, U. of Missouri - Rolla, U. of Missouri - St. Louis, U. of Missouri-kansas city, U. of MN, U. of Montana, U. of Montreal, U. of MS, Oxford, U. of Muenster, U. of munich, U. of Nantes (France), U. of Nebraska-Lincoln, U. of Nebraska-Omaha, U. Of Nevada, U. of nevada reno, U. of Nevada, Las Vegas, U. of Nevada, Reno, U. of nevada,reno, U. of New Brunswick, U. of new hampshire, U. of new mexico, U. of new orleans, U. of New South Wales, U. of Newcastle Upon Tyne, U. of Newcastle, Australia, U. of Nijmegen, U. of North Texas, U. of Northern Colorado, U. of Northumbria, UK, U. of Notre Dame, U. of Nottingham, UK, U. of Oklahoma, U. of Oklahoma, Norman, OK, U. of Oregon, U. of Oslo, Norway, U. of otago, U. of Otago, Dunedin, New Zealand, U. of Otago, New Zealand, U. of Ottawa, U. of Oulu, U. of Oxford, U. of Paris 5, U. of Passau, Germany, U. of Penn, U. of Pennsylvania, U. of Peradeniya, U. of Pierre and Marie curie - Paris VI - France, U. of Pittsburg, U. of Pretoria (South Africa), U. of Prince Edward Island, U. of Puerto Rico, U. of Puget Sound, U. of Pune, U. of QLD, U. of Queensland, Australia, U. Of Rajasthan, U. of Reading, U. of Regensburg, Germany, U. of Regina, U. of Regina, SK, Canada, U. of Reims, U. of Rhode Island, U. of richmond, U. of Rochester, U. of S. Carolina, U. of Saarland, Germany, U. Of Salford, U. of Sao Paulo - Brazil, U. of Saskatchewan, U. of Seville, U. of Sheffield, U. of Sheffield, UK, U. of Sherbrooke, U. of Skovde, U. of South Alabama, U. of South Australia, U. of South Carolina, U. of South Florida, U. of southampton, U. of Southampton, UK, U. of Southern California, U. of Southern Denmark, U. of Southern Mississippi, U. of St. Andrews, U. of Stelenbosch, U. of Stellenbosch, South Africa, U. of Strathclyde, U. of Stuttgart / Germany, U. of surrey, U. of Surrey, UK, U. of sydney, U. of Tartu, U. of Tasmania, U. of Technology, Sydney (UTS), U. of Tehran, U. of Tennessee, U. of Texas, U. of Texas - Houston, U. of Texas - Pan American, U. of Texas (Austin), U. of Texas at Dallas, U. of Texas at El Paso, U. of Texas at San Antonio, U. of the federal armed Forces Munich, U. OF THE INCARNATE WORD, U. of the Philippines, Diliman, U. of the Punjab, U. of the West of England, U. of Tokyo, U. of Toledo, U. of Toulon (France), U. of Trier, U. of Twente, the Netherlands, U. of Ulm, U. of Ulster, U. of Umea, U. of Utah, U. of Utrecht, U. of VA, U. of Vermont, U. of Victoria, U. of Vienna, U. of Virginia, U. of Würzburg, U. of Waikato, NZ, U. of Wales, Bangor, UK, U. of Warwick, UK, U. of Washington, U. of Waterloo, Ontario, Canada, U. of West Bohemia, U. of West Florida, U. of West Georgia, U. of Western Australia, U. of Western Ontario, U. of Western Sydney, U. of westminster, U. of Windsor, U. of Winnipeg, U. of Wisconsin-Madison, U. of Wollongong, Australia, U. of Wuerzburg, Germany, U. of York, UK, U. of Zagreb, Croatia, U. of Zurich, U. Oporto, U. Saarland, U. Technology Malaysia, U. Tenaga Nasional, U., Poland, U. of California, Irvine, U. of Houston, University at buffalo, universtiy at buffalo, Universtiy of Houston, Universtiy of Saskatchewan, Universtiy of Texas, Universite de Geneve, University of Copenhagen/Technical U. of De, University of Queensland, AUS, University of Wisconsin-Madison, U. of Washington, Unv Evora, UP Diliman, Philippines, Uppsala U., Sweden, Ursinus College, US Army, Iraq, USAF Academy, USC (South Carolina), utah state U., Utrecht U., Valdosta State U., Vanderbilt U., Vassar College, Vaxjo U., Veterinary School, Universitat Autònoma Barcelona, victor valley college, Victoria U of Tech, Victoria U. of Wellington, Vidyaranya High School For Boys And Girls, Vienna Medical School, Vienna U. of Technology, villanova, Virginia Commonwealth U. virginia institute of marine science, Virginia Polytechnic and State U., Virginia Tech U., Viveka, Vrije U. Amsterdam, VUB Belgium, Wake Forest, Walden U., Warsaw U. of Technology, Warw, Warwick, Warwick U., Wash U in St. Louis, washburn U., washington, Washington State U., Washington U., Waterloo Wayne State U., Wayne State U. School of Medicine, Wellesley College, Wesleyan U., West Virginia U., Western Illinois U., Western Kentucky U., Western Washington U., westlake high school, Westminster College, Westmont, Wharton School, wheaton, Wichita State U., wilfrid laurier U., Wilkes U., William Clarke College, William Jewell College, William Paterson U., williamsville north, windsor, winthrop U., Wollongong Uni, Australia, Worcester Polytechnic Institute, worcester state college, WPI, Wright State U., Xavier Institute of Communications, Xavier U., Yale U., Yonsei U., York U., Yousei U. Yuan Ze U. This is a list of the schools of the people who subscribe to www.phdcomics.com, sampled in 2005. Duplicates were checked for through "direct experimentation."

This one's for the fans

COMIC STRIPS
2005-2007

DESK ENTROPY

Definition

Desk entropy is a spatiodynamic quantity that measures a workspace's degree of disorder, and the inability to find anything when you really need it.

Any spontaneous activity, whether productive or unproductive, disperses crap matter and increases overall desk entropy.

Efforts to reverse desk entropy are temporary, and inevitably decrease over time.

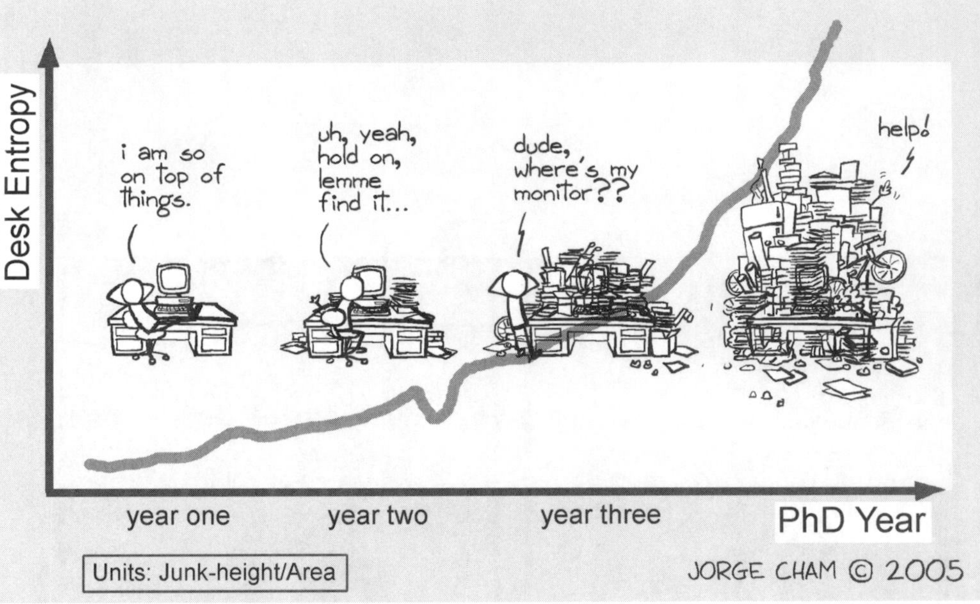

HEY, WHAT ARE YOU WATCHING?

JORGE CHAM © 2005

DOES IT MATTER?
BAD DAY, HUH?

TV SHOWS ARE ALWAYS ABOUT DOCTORS, COPS OR LAWYERS. WHAT ABOUT US?
WHERE'S A SHOW I CAN RELATE TO?

I FEEL TOTALLY IGNORED BY POP CULTURE!
WHY CAN'T THEY MAKE A SHOW ABOUT GRAD STUDENTS?
JORGE CHAM © 2005

BECAUSE ALL WE EVER DO IS SIT AROUND AND COMPLAIN?
WE HAVE DOCTORS TOO!

THEY SHOULD TOTALLY MAKE A TV SHOW ABOUT GRAD STUDENTS.
I'D WATCH IT!
I DON'T KNOW...

PEOPLE LIKE SHOWS ABOUT DOCTORS AND COPS BECAUSE THEY INVOLVE LIFE OR DEATH SITUATIONS.
JORGE CHAM © 2005

OUR SITUATIONS BARELY QUALIFY AS LIFE.
you could do a whole episode on data analysis!

THAT WAS A GREAT CLASS!
YEAH!
SO REFRE-SHING!
I KNOW!
I FEEL ENERGI-ZED!
ME TOO!

YOU WERE ASLEEP THE WHOLE TIME, WEREN'T YOU?
WEREN'T YOU?
JORGE CHAM © 2007

DID YOU STAY UP LATE?
NO.
GET UP EARLY?
NO.
SO WHAT HAPPENED?
I NEED A REASON?

WHY DO YOU EVEN COME TO CLASS?
WELL, IT'D BE RUDE NOT TO AT LEAST SHOW UP!

The NEW Grad School Food Pyramid

Steps to a cheaper you

www.phdcomics.com

Healthy foods
Fruits, veggies.
Use sparingly.

Caffeinated foods
chocolate, coffee.
10-20 servings/day

Cheap foods you eat from a bowl
Ramen, cereal.
3-5 servings/day

Free foods
Pizza, cookies, chips.
As many servings as possible.

Zzzz

RAMEN

SUGAR FLAKES

JORGE CHAM © 2005

The USDA is proud to present updated guidelines to better grad eating. The new GradPyramid™ is designed to encourage dietary choices that promote productivity, reduce the risk of major chronic laziness, and allow stipends to remain at a minimum.

Free food doesn't fit all. The new GradPyramid recommends different proportions of the four basic food groups depending on your stage in the PhD process:

First years: take advantage of over-abundant Free Foods, but vary your pizza topping intake. Avoid cookies with raisins (it's fruit in disguise).

Years 2-3: Maintain a steady diet of sugar and caffeine for late night quals study sessions. Go easy on sleep, and limit daylight.

Years 4 and over: Aging bodies and empty wallets make bowl foods right for you. Choose cereals with cartoon characters on box and ramen sold in bulk. Be physically active at least once.

CECILIA, YOU CAN'T JUST IGNORE YOUR BIRTHDAY!
NO? I'VE DECIDED THAT MY YEARS IN GRAD SCHOOL DO NOT COUNT TOWARDS MY TOTAL AGE.

HAVE I GROWN AS A PERSON IN GRAD SCHOOL?
HAVE I REALLY MATURED?
MY LIFE HAS BEEN ON PAUSE EVER SINCE I GOT HERE, IT'S ONLY FAIR I DON'T GET OLDER EITHER.
JORGE CHAM © 2005

HUH. YOU'VE TAKEN IT TO A WHOLE NEW LEVEL. YOU'RE PRO-CRASTINATING TIME ITSELF!
if only that worked for the weight gained in grad school, too.

WHEN I WAS LITTLE, I THOUGHT MY LIFE WOULD BE SET AT AGE 25...

I'D HAVE A JOB, BE MARRIED, HAVE KIDS...
25 SEEMED SO FAR AWAY, MY LIFE PLAN DIDN'T EVEN COVER WHAT HAPPENS AFTER.

JORGE CHAM © 2005

I GUESS YOU NEED A NEW PLAN.
I NEED A NEW PLAN!!

ADDRESSING REVIEWER COMMENTS

BAD REVIEWS ON YOUR PAPER? FOLLOW THESE GUIDE-LINES AND YOU MAY YET GET IT PAST THE EDITOR:

Reviewer comment:

"The method/device/paradigm the authors propose is clearly wrong."

How NOT to respond:

✗ "Yes, we know. We thought we could still get a paper out of it. Sorry."

Correct response:

✓ "The reviewer raises an interesting concern. However, as the focus of this work is exploratory and not performance-based, validation was not found to be of critical importance to the contribution of the paper."

Reviewer comment:

"The authors fail to reference the work of Smith et al., who solved the same problem 20 years ago."

How NOT to respond:

✗ "Huh. We didn't think anybody had read that. Actually, their solution is better than ours."

Correct response:

✓ "The reviewer raises an interesting concern. However, our work is based on completely different first principles (we use different variable names), and has a much more attractive graphical user interface.

Reviewer comment:

"This paper is poorly written and scientifically unsound. I do not recommend it for publication."

How NOT to respond:

✗ "You #&@*% reviewer! I know who you are! I'm gonna get you when it's my turn to review!"

Correct response:

✓ "The reviewer raises an interesting concern. However, we feel the reviewer did not fully comprehend the scope of the work, and misjudged the results based on incorrect assumptions.

MEETING OF THE MINDS...
HE'S TOTALLY ON TO ME. HE KNOWS I'VE DONE NOTHING THIS WEEK!
I CAN SEE IT IN HIS DISAPPROVING EYES, HE THINKS I'M WORTHLESS!
UH, SO... UH...
HMMM.
I SEE.
INTERESTING.
HMM, SQUASH GAME WITH PROF. JONES TODAY, THAT OLD BUGGER.
WHICH REMINDS ME, GOTTA PICK UP THE DRY CLEANING.
AND WHAT'S THIS GUY'S NAME AGAIN?
JORGE CHAM © 2005

I'M OFF TO CLASS, SEE YOU-
WHAT?

IS THAT WHAT YOU'RE GOING TO WEAR?
YES...

FRUMPY SWEATER, BAGGY SWEATPANTS AND WHITE TENNIS SHOES?
I SHOULD WEAR A HAT, HUH?
JORGE CHAM © 2005

IN ENGINEERING, A GIRL HAS TO DRESS TO REPRESS.
excuse me, female, will you marry me?

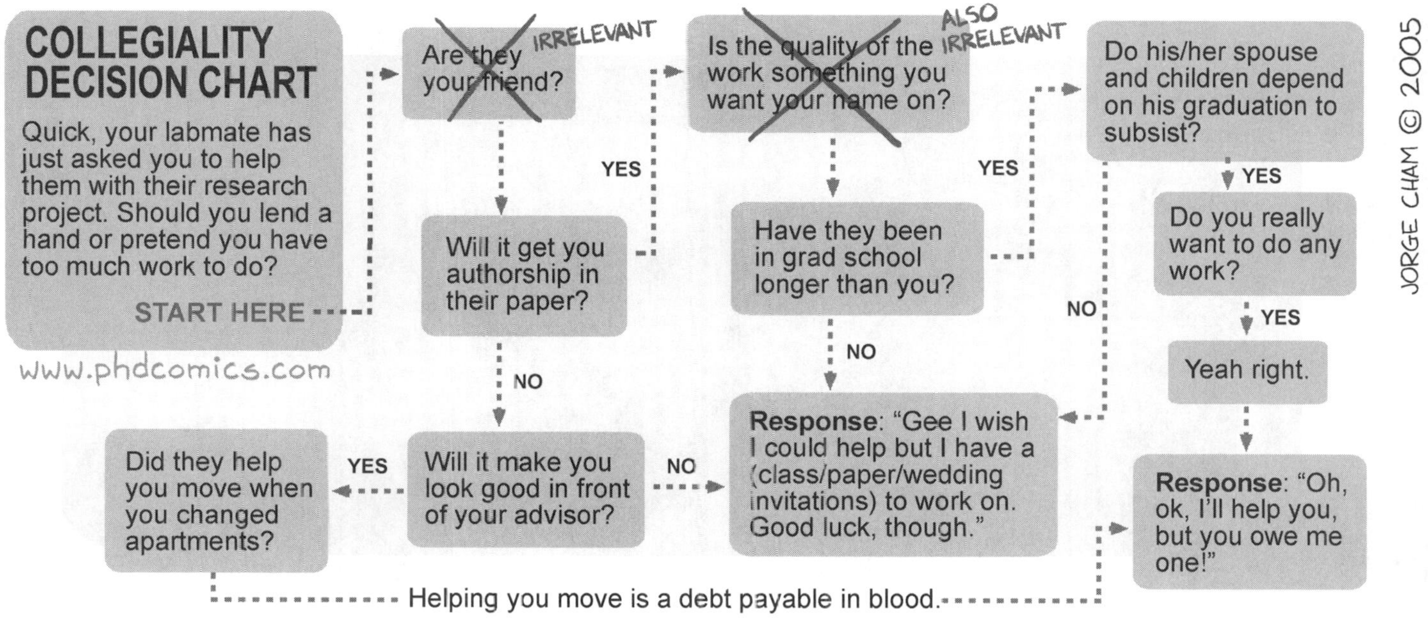

COLLEGIALITY DECISION CHART

Quick, your labmate has just asked you to help them with their research project. Should you lend a hand or pretend you have too much work to do?

START HERE → Are they your friend? (crossed out: IRRELEVANT)

↓ Will it get you authorship in their paper?
- YES → Is the quality of the work something you want your name on? (crossed out: ALSO IRRELEVANT)
  ↓ Have they been in grad school longer than you?
  - YES → Do his/her spouse and children depend on his graduation to subsist?
    - YES → Do you really want to do any work?
      - YES → Yeah right. → Response: "Oh, ok, I'll help you, but you owe me one!"
    - NO → Response: "Gee I wish I could help but I have a (class/paper/wedding invitations) to work on. Good luck, though."
  - NO → Response: "Gee I wish I could help but I have a (class/paper/wedding invitations) to work on. Good luck, though."
- NO → Will it make you look good in front of your advisor?
  - NO → Response: "Gee I wish I could help but I have a (class/paper/wedding invitations) to work on. Good luck, though."
  - YES → Did they help you move when you changed apartments?
    - Helping you move is a debt payable in blood. → Response: "Oh, ok, I'll help you, but you owe me one!"

www.phdcomics.com

JORGE CHAM © 2005

IT'S... IT'S SNOWING.
IN JUNE.
I FEEL A GREAT DISTURBANCE IN THE FORCE!

MEANWHILE, IN HELL:
brrr.
JORGE CHAM © 2005

TO BE HONEST, MIKE, I NEVER THOUGHT THIS DAY WOULD COME.
ME NEITHER.

THE PHD IS A PATHWAY TO MANY ABILITIES SOME CONSIDER...
UN-NATURAL.

YES... GIVE IN TO YOUR RESEARCH...
IT IS...
...YOUR DESTINY!

RISE, MY APPRENTICE...
HENCEFORTH, YOU SHALL BE KNOWN AS...
DR. SLACK-ENERNY!
JORGE CHAM © 2005

EPISODE III: REVENGE OF THE SMITH.
NOOOOOO!!
hehehe...

Once upon a time...
On a campus far far away...

There lived a most unhappy grad student...
...whom everyone called, er, Cingradella.
JORGE CHAM © 2005

Cingradella was unhappy because her advisor had gone on sabbatical...
...and left her in the care of an evil post-doc, who disliked Cingradella's experimental methods very much.

IS THAT ALL YOU GRAD STUDENTS CAN TALK ABOUT?
RESEARCH?
LISTEN, YOU WANT A STORY OR NOT?
BOOO-RING!

Cingradella had two lazy labmates, who were favored by her evil post-doc, and together they delighted in making Cingradella do all of the lab's drudgery...

cleaning the community kitchen...
giving lab tours...

and maintaining the lab's file and e-mail server.
JORGE CHAM © 2005
WHAT A SAP!
SUCH WAS HER LOT IN LIFE...

One day, a royal e-mail arrived announcing a prestigious workshop organized by Prof. Charles Ming...

for Prof. Ming was a renowned expert in their field

And though years in grad school had accustomed her to injustice and disappointment...

...but Cingradella knew they would not send her.

...and every grad student in the kingdom wanted to work with him.

...a single tear escaped from her eye.

As the tear fell upon her keyboard, a magical creature suddenly appeared!

"Who are you?" asked Cingradella.

"I am your Fairy Grad Mentor!" said the emeritus faculty, "I am here to make all your wishes come true!"

- "ALL my wishes?" asked Cingradella.
- "Well, actua-" said the fairy.
- "Can you make me graduate?"
- "Um, anything except that."
- "But you said-"
- "Look kid, i said wishes, not miracles!"

With a wave of the fairy's wand, the clothes Cingradella had been wearing since undergrad transformed into the latest in "casual academic"!

"But how can I go? I have nothing to present!" said Cingradella.

"I give to you this glass thesis. Like all theses, it is shiny and pretty, but transparent and fragile, and you must bring it back by mid-night." replied the fairy.

JORGE CHAM © 2005

"Why mid-night?" exclaimed Cingradella, as she sped away in an undergrad-drawn ramen bowl carriage.

"That's when another group publishes results that disprove it. Have a good time!"

At the workshop, Cingradella generated a buzz among the attendees...

...and many courted her with grant proposals.

Her talk was the most well received of all the talks, and caught the attention of Prof. Charles Ming...

...but as she began to take questions, the clock struck mid-night: her talk had run over!

Hurriedly, she packed her things and rushed to her ramen carriage...

...leaving behind the glass thesis the fairy had given her.

JORGE CHAM © 2005

Charles Ming searched all throughout the kingdom for the one responsible for the glass thesis...

YEAH, YEAH, LET ME GUESS...

HE FINDS CINGRADELLA AND ALL HER WISHES COME TRUE.

ACTUALLY...

Just then, Cingradella's advisor returned! "I should have known YOU were behind this brilliant work, Prof. Jones!" said Charles Ming, "Let's collaborate!"

...until finally he arrived in the laboratory where Cingradella worked.

JORGE CHAM © 2005

For the moral of our story is: though grad students may do all the work, it is their advisors that get all the glory.

AWKWARD PLACES TO RUN INTO YOUR ADVISOR

WELL, ONE GOOD THING ABOUT WORKING IN THE BASEMENT...
IT'S ALWAYS NICE AND COOL DOWN HERE.

PEOPLE UP THERE MUST BE ROASTING RIGHT NOW UNDER THE HEAT OF THE NOON SUMMER SUN.
JORGE CHAM © 2005

DUDE, IT'S 3am, NOT NOON.
CURSE YOU WINDOWLESS EXISTENCE!!

CAN YOU BELIEVE THEY GAVE THE GUY WHO DRAWS THAT "FOXTROT" COMIC STRIP AN HONO-RARY PH.D?
SO?

SO, IT'S OUT OF CONTROL!
HERE WE ARE, SLAVING AWAY IN GRAD SCHOOL...
...AND THEY JUST GIVE IT AWAY TO SOME CARTOO-NIST!

HOW MANY PEOPLE READ HIS COMIC?
UH, MILLIONS.
HOW MANY ARE GOING TO READ YOUR THESIS?
BESIDES ME?
JORGE CHAM © 2005

OK, NOBODY.
SO WHO'S SMARTER NOW?
WELL, AT LEAST IT WAS ONLY A HU-MANITIES PH.D.
what do y... HEY!

PHD ZEN

If you want to write a thesis...

...start with the acknowledgments.

What is the sound...

...of no hands typing?

If a grad student falls asleep in the lab, and no one is there to see her...

...is she still goofing off?

DID YOU GET THAT EMAIL FROM PROF. SMITH?
UH... NO.
REALLY? HE SENT IT TO EVERYONE.
I GUESS MY SPAM FILTER MUST HAVE DELETED IT.

THAT'S WEIRD. WHAT ARE YOUR SPAM SETTINGS?
I USE A VERY STRICT SET OF KEYWORD HEU-RISTICS BASED ON SUBJECT MATTER
JORGE CHAM © 2005

LET ME GUESS, ANYTHING THAT DOESN'T SAY "FREE FOOD" GETS DELETED?
IF IT'S NOT ABOUT FOOD, IT'S UNSO-LICITED.

GOODNESS, WHAT A SCORCHER TODAY!
I KNOW! IT'S SO HOT IT'S UNBEARABLE!

YOU'D THINK A PLACE THAT PRIDES ITSELF ON TECHNOLOGY WOULD HAVE BETTER A/C.
THE HEAT, THE STRAIN, THE HARD LABOR...
JORGE CHAM © 2005

...NOW IT **REALLY** FEELS LIKE WE'RE IN HELL.
GRAD SCHOOL, ETERNAL DAMNATION... WHAT'S THE DIFFERENCE?

SO... HOT...
CAN'T...

FWOOSH!!

...AND THEN IT BURST INTO FLAMES!
OBVIOUSLY, YOU'VE BEEN WORKING TOO HARD.
TAKE THE REST OF THE SUM-MER OFF.
PROF JONES
JORGE CHAM © 2005

THE HEAT FINALLY GOT TO HER...
thanks... prof. jones...

AH, THE SUMMER MONTHS...
THE PERFECT TIME TO GET RESEARCH DONE.

NO CLASSES
NO DISTRACTIONS
NO INTERRUPTIONS
JORGE CHAM © 2005

NO EXCUSES
I'M MEETING PROF. SMITH IN FIVE MINUTES
AND I HAVE NOTHING TO SHOW!
dude, you're on your own.

HEY.
HEY.

UH, ARE YOU WAITING FOR PROF. SMITH?
YEAH.
LOOKS LIKE HE DOUBLE-BOOKED US.
JORGE CHAM © 2005

BUT WE SCHEDULED MY MEETING WEEKS AGO!
YEAH, WELL...
JOIN THE CLUB.
NEXT!
you go first.

SO, DO **YOU** HAVE ANYTHING TO SHOW PROF. SMITH?
NEXT!
UH... NO.

NO NEW DATA?
NOPE.
NEED HIS ADVICE ON ANYTHING?
NOT REALLY.
JORGE CHAM © 2005

AFRAID IF YOU DON'T MEET WITH HIM, HE'LL FORGET YOU EXIST?
i only bring these to keep my hands from trembling.
NEXT!

YOU MEAN TO TELL ME THAT YOU HAVEN'T DONE ANYTHING ALL SUMMER??
I OUGHT TO...
brrring!
HOLD ON.

UH HUH.
UH HUH.
NO NO, CHANNEL THE MONEY THROUGH THE DISCRETIONARY FUND.
ALLRIGHT.

SORRY ABOUT THAT. NOW, WHERE WERE WE?
UH...
JORGE CHAM © 2005

WE WERE JUST WRAPPING UP?
OH.
WELL, SEE YOU NEXT WEEK THEN.
NEXT!
SOMETIMES, THEIR FORGETFULNESS HAS ITS ADVANTAGES.

NEXT!
PHEW, THAT WAS CLOSE.

THAT'S IT. NO MORE FOOLING AROUND.
I AM GOING TO CATCH UP ON RESEARCH THIS WEEK AND SHOW PROF. SMITH I AM **NOT** A SLACKER!
AIEEEE!!
JORGE CHAM © 2005

ONE WEEK LATER:
I'M MEETING PROF. SMITH IN FIVE MINUTES...
AND I HAVE NOTHING TO SHOW!

YOUR ADVISOR IS ON VACATION. HOW TO REACT:

YEAR 1 GRAD:

YEAR 3 GRAD:

YEAR 5 GRAD:

YEAR 7 GRAD:

WELCOME BACK TO THE SHOW!

the WILEY SPRINGER SHOW

Today: Lyin' labmates!

WHOO! CLAP CLAP CLAP C LAP CLAP CL

WITH US HERE TODAY IS JOHNNY...

NOW, YOU'RE A FIRST YEAR, ISN'T THAT RIGHT, JOHNNY?

Y-YES, WILEY.

TELL US, WHY ARE YOU HERE, JOHNNY?

WILEY SPRINGER JOHNNY has secret to reveal

I... I HAVE A CONFESSION TO MAKE...

TO MY LABMATE.

JORGE CHAM © 2005

JOHNNY HERE HAS A CONFESSION TO MAKE TO HIS LABMATE.
GO AHEAD, JOHNNY.
UM, WELL, WHEN I FIRST JOINED THE GROUP...
YES..?
...I WAS ASSIGNED TO YOUR PROJECT.
I'VE BEEN RUNNING YOUR EXPERIMENTS, CRUNCHING YOUR NUMBERS, CLEANING YOUR EQUIPMENT...
YES, YOU'VE BEEN A GOOD LACKEY.
WELL, I... I CAN'T KEEP THIS A SECRET ANYMORE...
I'M SEEING ANOTHER GRAD STUDENT.
WHAT THE BEEEP!?
BEEP BEE BEEEEP!
OOOHH!
JORGE CHAM © 2005
YOU'RE SWITCHING TO ANOTHER GRAD STUDENT'S PROJECT?
AFTER ALL THE WORK I LET YOU DO FOR ME?
I...
I WAS GOING TO INCLUDE YOU IN MY ACKNOWLEDGMENTS!
WE DIDN'T MEAN FOR THIS TO HAPPEN!
WHO? WHO IS IT?
YOUR OFFICE-MATE.
OOOHH!
WE HAVE HER HERE IN THE STUDIO, BRING HER OUT!
YOU!
FIRST YOU STEAL MY STAPLER, AND NOW MY LACKEY!?
OH YEAH, YOU BEEP BEEEP
WHY YOU BEEEEP B BEEEP
WE'LL BE RIGHT BACK.
JORGE CHAM © 2005

...AND WE'RE BACK. JOHNNY HERE HAS JUST CONFESSED...
...HE'S THROUGH BEING A LACKEY FOR RUSSELL, AND NOW WORKS FOR MARY, RUSSELL'S OFFICE-MATE. LET'S HEAR FROM THE AUDIENCE.
YEAH, TO THE YOUNG DUDE: YOU GO, MAN, YOU DON'T OWE NOTHIN' TO NOBODY...
AND TO THE DUDE WITH THE PONY TAIL: AIN'T NOBODY TOLD YOU PONY TAILS WENT OUTTA STYLE AGES AGO?

HAHA, HE'S JUST MAKING UP FOR HIS RECEDING HAIRLINE!
WHATEVER, I'M NOT THE ONE WHO BLASTS CHEESY 80'S MUSIC IN THE OFFICE ALL DAY!

YEAH? WELL AT LEAST I SHOWER ON A REGULAR BASIS!
WHY YOU BEEEEP
FIGHT! FIGHT! WHOOOO!

YOU'RE THE WORST OFFICEMATE I'VE EVER HAD!
ME!? YOUR MESS TAKES UP HALF THE OFFICE, AND YOU YAK ON THE PHONE ALL DAY!

STOP! CAN'T YOU SEE? MARY CAN GIVE ME SOME-THING YOU CAN'T...
FUNDING.

WAIT, WHAT?
YOUR FELLOWSHIP RAN OUT?
OOOHH...

PFFT, LIKE I'M GOING TO SHARE MY GRANT WITH HIM...
LET'S DITCH THE LOSER AND GET SOME COFFEE
I'M SURE THERE'S A LESSON HERE SOMEWHERE.
TOMORROW ON OUR SHOW: ADVISORS GONE WILD!

HEY, WHAT'S U-
OH, NO YOU DON'T.

WHAT?
YOU DON'T WANT TO WORK, SO YOU'RE PROWLING FOR VICTIMS TO PROCRASTI-NATE WITH.

WELL, YOU'RE NOT SUCKING ME INTO YOUR VORTEX OF UNPRODUCTIVITY.
I HAVE WORK TO DO.
JORGE CHAM © 2005

I HEAR THERE'S A NEW CANDY AT THE VENDING MACHINE.
DARN YOU, LET'S GO.

YO.
S'UP.

JORGE CHAM © 2005

ALLRIGHT. LET'S GO.
THE VORTEX GROWS.

LIKE A BLACK HOLE, THE VORTEX OF UNPRODUCTIVITY SUCKS EVERYTHING IN ITS PATH...
hey, where's everyone g—
uh oh.

GAINING MOMENTUM, ITS GRAVITATIONAL PULL INCREASES...
no! i got work to do!
prof. smith is going to fire me if i don't—!
yo.
s'up.
JORGE CHAM © 2005

THE WILL TO WORK GOES IN... NOTHING COMES OUT!
he can't fire ALL of us, can he?
so... what are we doing?
NOTHING!

THE VORTEX REACHES CRITICAL MASS...
HEY, WHAT ARE YOU DOING?

GUILT BEGINS TO STRAIN THE SYSTEM.
UH, JUST CHECKING EMAIL.
YEAH, I SHOULD GET BACK TO WORK.
YEAH.
ME TOO.
JORGE CHAM © 2005

THE BUBBLE OF UNPRODUCTIVITY COLLAPSES.
HEY, WHERE DID EVERYBODY GO?

```
% phd.m
%
% author: Cecilia
% date: 09/08/05

load THESIS_TOPIC

while (funding==true)
    data = run_experiment(THESIS_TOPIC);
    GOOD_ENOUGH = query(advisor);
    if (data > GOOD_ENOUGH)
        graduate();
        break
    else
        THESIS_TOPIC = new();
        years_in_gradschool += 1;
    end
end
```

SUMMER'S OVER, DEE. WE GOT CLASS IN FIVE MINUTES.
JUST LET ME KNOW WHEN IT'S TIME FOR MIDTERMS.
JORGE CHAM © 2005

JORGE CHAM © 2005

HEY, WHAT ARE ROOM-MATES FOR?
THANKS.

UM, SO THEN THE OPTIMIZATION SHOWS A NEGATIVE TREND IN THE DATA THAT...
UH HUH... UH HUH.
DO YOU PLAY SQUASH?

I... WHAT?
SQUASH. DO YOU PLAY? I NEED A NEW PARTNER.
JORGE CHAM © 2005

ACTUALLY, I DON'T-
SPLENDID! WE'LL PLAY TOMORROW.
HOPEFULLY, YOU CAN DODGE A RACKET BETTER THAN MY LAST PARTNER.

please don't show up, please don't show up.
AH, THERE YOU ARE!
darn.

READY FOR SOME FRIENDLY GENTLEMANLY SPORT?
HEY, PROF. SMITH
NOW, DON'T HOLD BACK JUST BECAUSE I'M YOUR ADVISOR...

...BUT I WARN YOU: IF I DON'T WIN, YOU'RE FIRED.
JORGE CHAM © 2005

HA, I'M KIDDING.
ha-ha... FUNNY, SIR.
i'm gonna wipe the floor with you. there's no way you can beat me.
help me stretch, will you?

NOW REMEMBER, THERE'S NO SHAME IN LOSING TO A PRO.
uh, GOT IT, SIR.
HERE WE GO.

$#%@!!

GGAAAARRGHH! @$%#& *%$#@!!
JORGE CHAM © 2005

HMPH. WELL, PLAYED.
your serve.

RRAAARGH!
BEATING PROF. SMITH CAN'T BE GOOD FOR MY CAREER.
I'LL JUST MISS THIS SHOT AND LET HIM WIN.

JORGE CHAM © 2005

AAAH!! PROF. SMITH, ARE YOU ALLRIGHT??
...
QUICK, WHAT'S MY NAME?
...
OK, NEVER MIND.

PROF. SMITH??
WHAT'S... WHAT'S THE SCORE?

UH... YOU'RE... WINNING, SIR.
BY ONE POINT.
I AM?
I MEAN...

WILL YOU LOOK AT THE TIME? I HAVE TO GO, UH, PICK UP MY KIDS.
JORGE CHAM © 2005

NOW DON'T TAKE IT SO BAD. AT LEAST YOU HAVE PLENTY OF YEARS HERE LEFT TO PRACTICE.
let's hit the showers.
YES, SIR.

HEY, WHERE YOU BEEN?
OH MAN, I JUST PLAYED SQUASH WITH PROF. SMITH.
YOU WHAT?

YOU DID SOMETHING WITH PROF. SMITH OUTSIDE THE LAB?
HE'S NEVER ASKED ME TO PLAY SQUASH WITH HIM.
DUDE, YOU'RE TOTALLY HIS FAVORITE.
JORGE CHAM © 2005

HOW WAS IT?
I ALMOST KILLED HIM AND HAD TO WATCH HIM CHANGE CLOTHES.
WELL, GOOD LUCK WITH THAT.
BETTER YOU THAN ME.
BROWN-NOSER.

type type
(save)
type type
(save)

type type
(save)
type
(save)

(save)
type
(save)
type
(save)
JORGE CHAM © 2005

A LITTLE OVERCAUTIOUS, DON'T YOU THINK?
WHAT DO YOU
(save)
MEAN?

DO YOU REALLY NEED TO SAVE THAT OFTEN?
EVERY SENTENCE DESERVES A GOOD SAVE.

I ALSO SAVE TO A BACKUP DRIVE, FLASH MEMORY, MY HOME COMPUTER, PRINT HARD COPIES EVERY TWO HOURS,
AND A SERVER CLUSTER IN NORWAY.
JORGE CHAM © 2005

LIVING ON THE EDGE, ARE WE?
"BETTER SAFE THAN EVEN-SORRIER-YOU-CAME-TO-GRAD-SCHOOL," I ALWAYS SAY.

CECILIA, YOU CAN'T SPEND HALF YOUR LIFE BACKING EVERY-THING UP.
MAYBE I **HAVE** BEEN PLAYING IT TOO SAFE...

I MEAN, WHAT ARE THE CHANCES THAT A SIMPLE COMPUTER GLITCH OR VIRUS WILL DELETE EVERYTHING YOU'VE DONE?
WHAT WOULD BE SO BAD ABOUT...

...**STARTING ALL OVER** AGAIN?
er... i gotta go, uh, check on something. be right back.
JORGE CHAM © 2005

it's not paranoia if you're always right.

FIRE DOOR
KEEP CLOSED

FIRE DOOR
KEEP CLOSED

JORGE CHAM © 2005

FIRE DOOR
KEEP CLOSED

YOU KNOW, I HAVEN'T SEEN MIKE IN A WHILE.
WHAT'S THAT?

MIKE. I DON'T THINK HE'S COME INTO WORK IN MONTHS. ISN'T THAT FUNNY?
HUH.
I HADN'T NOTICED.

HA.
THAT MIKE...
heh.
JORGE CHAM © 2005
YOU THINK ANYONE WOULD NOTICE IF I DIDN'T SHOW UP?
THIS IS GRAD SCHOOL. THEY'LL NOTICE FURNITURE MISSING BEFORE THEY NOTICE YOU.

BEFORE WE BEGIN, I JUST WANT TO SAY...
THANK YOU.
JORGE CHAM © 2005

THANK YOU FOR BEING MY STUDENT, FOR SACRIFICING YOUR TIME TO FURTHER MY CAREER...
...IT IS AN HONOR TO BE YOUR ADVISOR.
prof. smith?

YOU... YOU DON'T KNOW HOW MUCH THAT MEANS TO ME, SIR... THANK YOU! THANK YOU!
NO, THANK YOU... SON.
SOB!

I KNOW YOU DON'T HAVE ENOUGH TO DO, SO GRADE THESE OVER THE HOLIDAY.
THANK YOU. SIR.

CECILIA, YOU STAYED IN THE LAB ALL WEEKEND?
I HAD A TURKEY SANDWICH.

WELL HERE, I SAVED THE BREAD-STICK WISHBONE FROM THE TOFU TURKEY I MADE.
MAKE A WISH.

snap!
JORGE CHAM © 2005

NOPE. STILL HERE.
maybe you do need animal sacrifice to graduate.

GOODNESS CECILIA, WHERE DID YOU GET THAT SHIRT, A DUMPSTER?
WHAT?

THIS SHIRT? IT WAS A FREEBIE. I'VE HAD IT SINCE FRESHMAN YEAR.
IT'S MY FAVORITE T-SHIRT.

I KEEP IT BECAUSE IT REMINDS ME OF A SIMPLER TIME, OF MY DREAM TO COME TO GRAD SCHOOL AND MAKE A DIF-FERENCE...
JORGE CHAM © 2005

WHAT HAPPENED TO THAT DREAM?
IT'S STAINED AND CRUM-BLING, JUST LIKE THIS SHIRT.

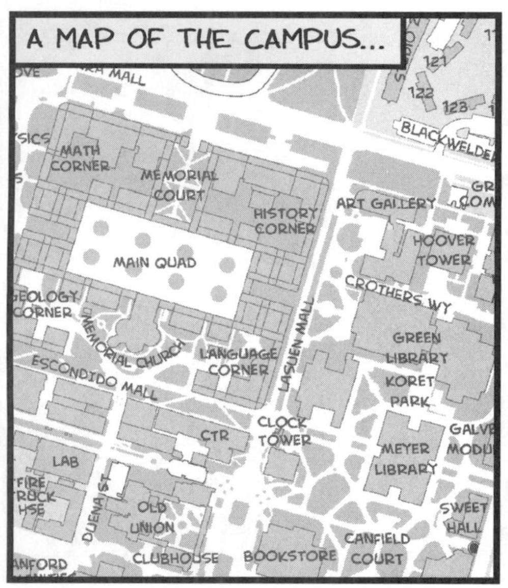
A MAP OF THE CAMPUS...
MATH CORNER
MEMORIAL COURT
HISTORY CORNER
ART GALLERY
BLACKWELDER
HOOVER TOWER
MAIN QUAD
CROTHERS WY
GEOLOGY CORNER
MEMORIAL CHURCH
LANGUAGE CORNER
LASUEN MALL
GREEN LIBRARY
ESCONDIDO MALL
KORET PARK
CLOCK TOWER
CTR
MEYER LIBRARY
LAB
FIRE TRUCK HSE
DUENA ST
OLD UNION
SWEET HALL
CANFIELD COURT
CLUBHOUSE
BOOKSTORE

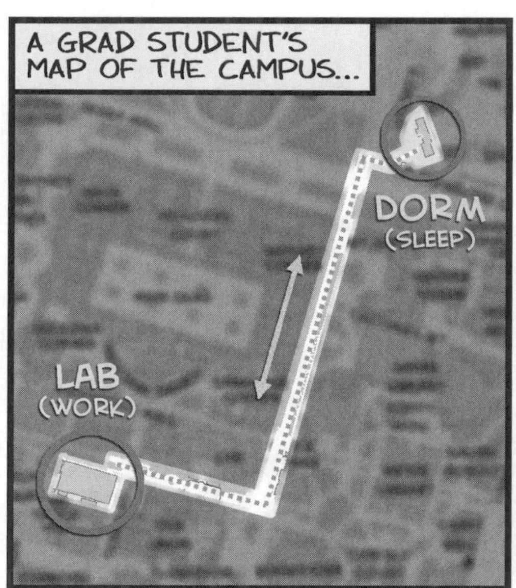
A GRAD STUDENT'S MAP OF THE CAMPUS...
DORM
(SLEEP)
LAB
(WORK)

EXCUSE ME, DO YOU KNOW WHERE THE PHYSICS BUILDING IS?
UH, SORRY. I'VE ONLY BEEN HERE FIVE YEARS.
MAP

BYE, PROF. SMITH!
HAVE A GOOD WINTER BREAK!
BAH.
LAZY GRAD STUDENTS.

IN MY DAY, I WOULD HAVE WORKED STRAIGHT THROUGH THE HOLIDAYS.
STILL... WITHOUT THEIR CONSTANT INEPTNESS TO INTERRUPT ME...
JORGE CHAM © 2005

I'M FINALLY FREE OF STUPID DIS-TRACTIONS.
oooOOooo OOHH..!
BEWARE!
phd presents
a smithmas carol
a winter break holiday special

"a smithmas carol" continues...
PROF. ZEKOWSKY?
MY OLD ADVISOR??
BUT YOU'RE... YOU'RE...
RETIRED?
YES.

DOOMED NOW TO WANDER THE HALLS OF ACADEMIA AS FACULTY EMERITUS ...
ONCE, I WAS HIGHLY RESPECTED FOR MY THEORIES...
JORGE CHAM © 2005

UNTIL SOMEBODY PROVED THEM ALL WRONG.
i should have let you rot in grad school...
YEAH... SORRY ABOUT THAT.

WELL, THANKS FOR STOPPING BY. NOW IF YOU'LL EXCUSE ME...
HEAR ME, SMITH! MY TIME IS NEARLY DONE.
I HAVE COME TO WARN YOU...

IT IS NOT TOO LATE FOR YOU!
YOU WILL BE VISITED BY THREE SPIRITS DURING YOUR OFFICE HOURS...
JORGE CHAM © 2005

BUT I'M NEVER HERE DURING "OFFICE HOURS"... IT'S JUST A DECOY TO THROW OFF STUDENTS.
OK, MAYBE IT IS TOO LATE FOR YOU.
WELL, SEE YOU AT THE NEXT CONFERENCE.

"a smithmas carol" continues...
knock knock.
COME IN!
HELLO?
AHEM.

I'M THE SPIRIT OF WINTER BREAK PAST BLAH BLAH BLAH...
LET'S GO. I'M A BUSY KID.
JORGE CHAM © 2005

WHERE ARE YOU TAKING M-
WAIT, I KNOW THIS PLACE...
oh man, prof. zekowski's going to kill me...
were sweater vests ever in style?

"a smithmas carol" continues...
WHY, THIS IS MY OLD LAB!
I HAVE SUCH FOND MEMORIES OF WORKING HERE!

THE HANDS-ON WORK, THE THRILL OF GATHERING DATA...
THE EXCITE-MENT OF DISCOVERY!
JORGE CHAM © 2005

AHH... TO BE A GRAD STUDENT AGAIN!

"a smithmas carol"
continues...
AND THERE I AM AS A GRAD STUDENT!
LOOK AT THAT WORK ETHIC!

I'M PROBABLY CONCENTRATING ON SOME DIFFI-CULT PROBLEM.
ANY SECOND NOW, A BRILLIANT SOLUTION WILL...
WILL...
JORGE CHAM © 2005
ZZZZZZ...
I'M JUST RESTING MY EYES.
I'M SURE.

"a smithmas carol"
continues...
HEY, BRIAN!
SANGEETA?
WELL, I'LL BE...

SANGEETA SINGH...
SHE HAD THE MOST ELEGANT NON-LINEAR VECTOR DERI-VATIONS...
i'm fine, how are... i mean, how's it go... i mean...
JORGE CHAM © 2005

NOT AS ELEGANT AS MINE, OF COURSE, BUT STILL, PRETTY GOOD.
OF COURSE.
uh, so...
so...

"a smithmas carol" continues...
HEY, I'M GOING DOWN TO THE DEPARTMENT HOLIDAY PARTY.
WANT TO COME WITH ME?
Y-YES! I'D LOVE TO...
BUT...

I HAVE TO STAY AND WORK.
NO! YOU FOOL!
oh.
JORGE CHAM © 2005

I KNOW, SHE SEEMED TO LIKE Y-
THERE'S A TYPO IN HIS EQUATION!
IT TOOK ME YEARS TO CATCH THAT SIGN ERROR!
well, see you around...
see you...

"a smithmas carol" continues...
great, now i can get back to wo-
knock knock!
PROF SMITH

HMM, THAT FEELING IN GRAD SCHOOL THAT YOUR ADVISOR IS WATCHING OVER YOU, JUDGING YOUR EVERY MOVE...
JORGE CHAM © 2005

...SOMEHOW FEELS MORE OMINOUS TODAY.
are you sure he's one of MY students?
i'm telling you..!

LOOK AT THAT POOR SOUL...
ALL ALONE ON CHRISTMAS DAY...

BURIED IN WORK...
TOO POOR TO FLY HOME FOR THE HO_IDAYS...
JORGE CHAM © 2005

HE'S PLAYING SOLITAIRE.
THAT'S EVEN SADDER!
darn. lost again.

deck the halls with lots of shirking fa lalalala lalala la!

'tis the reason we're not working fa lalalala lalala la!
JORGE CHAM © 2005

join us now in procras~tinating falalalala la la la laaaa..!

a smithmas carol continues...
knock knock...
OH, JUST COME IN...

GASP! THAT UNFORGIVING STARE...
THAT AURA OF DOOM...
A-ARE YOU...
JORGE CHAM © 2005

...PROF. LEVIN?
NO?
PROF. YANG? IS THAT YOU UNDER THAT HOOD?
are you sure?

a smithmas carol continues...
where are you tak-
WHO IS THIS NAME PLATE FOR?
SOME POOR FELLOW.

HE USED TO BE A FAMOUS RESEARCHER ONCE...
...BUT NOW HE JUST SITS IN MEETINGS AND FILLS OUT PAPERWORK.
?

JORGE CHAM © 2005
PROFESSOR SMITH
DEPARTMENT CHAIR
sigh...
NOOOO!!

GRAD HOROSCOPE

OUTLOOK FOR THE NEW YEAR

Mars and Jupiter's energies pose the question, "Are you in charge of your Destiny?" while Uranus' orbit chimes, "Don't be silly, you're in grad school."

BIOLOGY

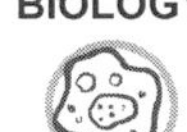

Your feelings of intellectual inadequacy will temporarily subside. Used to disappointment, you are willing to take chances despite risk of colossal rejection and embarrassment. Aim high, it will make failure easier to rationalize. Now is the time to submit that doomed paper to the journal Nature.

ECONOMICS

This is your year. Freakonomics and Angelina Jolie are making economists the hot geek of the moment. Take advantage of your enhanced sex appeal to remind your significant other that he/she did not make a mistake in going out with you. Once again, you will be asked by relatives for advice on their tax returns.

ENGINEERING

All your hard work will finally bear fruit. Resist temptation to eat that fruit, however, as all your results are based on simulation, not empirical data. This is a good year to learn new languages, like LaTeX.

ENGLISH

Doomed job prospects and increasing uncertainty regarding what your thesis actually accomplishes threaten your spirits. Channel your frustration on the undergrads you TA, except for the one that keeps flirting with you.

MATH

Your analytical abilities are at a high point, yet you will continue to squander them in grad school. Do not succumb to jealousy toward economists. Instead, focus your mathematical mind on good deeds or the stock market.

POLITICAL SCIENCE

Increasing outrage over the policies of your country's current administration will lead you to want to do something about it. Take the initiative and resist this urge, as it will only lead to more frustration. If you had any sort of leadership qualities, you wouldn't be in grad school.

JORGE CHAM © 2005

HOW'S THE DEBUGGING GOING?

YOU READY?
DUDE, WHAT'S WITH THE PINK SHORTS?
WHAT PINK SHORTS?

YOUR SHORTS, THEY'RE PINK.
WHAT ARE YOU TALKING ABOUT? I BOUGHT THESE MY FIRST YEAR.
THEY'RE RED!
JORGE CHAM © 2006

AREN'T THEY?
I'M SURPRISED THEY ACTUALLY FADED, GIVEN HOW RARELY YOU DO LAUNDRY.

HOW TO LOOK BUSY EVEN IF YOU'RE NOT

PART 3, MAINTAINING THE ILLUSION YOU'RE ALWAYS WORKING: TIMING YOUR EMAILS

SO...

JORGE CHAM © 2006

...WHAT'S NEW?
NOT MUCH, APPARENTLY.
ZZZZ

MIKE! YOU'RE BA-
WHOA...

DUDE, YOU'RE LIKE A... A... GROWN-UP, NOW.
MIKE SLACKEN-ERNY A FATHER...
JORGE CHAM © 2006

THINK SHE'LL GET HER PHD BEFORE HE DOES?
...she'll probably hood him. it'll be a touching ceremony.
HA HA. NOW GO AWAY, IT'S TIME FOR OUR NAP.

GOOD NEWS, CECILIA...
I HAVE A GOOD LEAD ON A FACULTY POSITION FOR YOU.
WHAT?

ME? A PROFESSOR?
OF COURSE, ISN'T THAT WHY YOU CAME TO GRAD SCHOOL?

JORGE CHAM © 2006

I DON'T KNOW, IS IT?
WELL, AT THIS POINT, IT'S THE ONLY JOB YOU'RE NOT OVERQUALIFIED FOR.

YOU'LL BE INVITED TO INTERVIEW, OF COURSE, BUT IT'S REALLY JUST A FORMALITY.

THE SEARCH COMMITTEE CHAIR AND I ALREADY DECIDED YOU AND THE FACULTY POSITION ARE A GOOD MATCH OF CALIBER, PEDIGREE AND RESEARCH INTERESTS...

PLUS, WE HIRED ONE OF THEIR GRADUATES LAST YEARS, SO DIPLOMATICALLY, THEY OWE US.
JORGE CHAM © 2006

IT'S NOT REALLY AN OPEN PROCESS. IT'S MORE LIKE AN ARRANGED MARRIAGE.
actually, "slave trade" came to mind first.

THE PHD GUIDE TO GROWN-UP CONVERSATIONS

HAVEN'T A CLUE WHAT YOUR FRIENDS WHO DIDN'T GO TO GRAD SCHOOL ARE TALKING ABOUT?

a PhD Valentine...
roses are red,
violets are blue
i'm so glad i found
a sugar-mama like you

you pay all our bills
you buy me nice things
you put up with my diet
of pizza, ramen and wings

i bet you didn't think
when we first infatuated
you'd have to wait years
for me to be graduated
JORGE CHAM © 2006

so thank you for dating
this geek
i love you to pieces
one day, you'll see
to you i'll dedicate my
thesis
allright, what did you do?

HEY, WHERE DID YOU GET THE CHOCOLATES?
THIS STUDENT IN THE CLASS I T.A. I THINK HE HAS A CRUSH ON ME.

HE GAVE YOU CHOCOLATE??
I KNOW, IT'S TOTALLY INAPPROPRIATE. I LET HIM DOWN EASY.

JORGE CHAM © 2006

BUT YOU KEPT THE CHOCOLATE?
HEY, A GIRL'S GOT TO EAT.

DEPARTMENT RECRUITMENT STATISTICS

HARD TO BELIEVE? NOT ACCORDING TO THE OFFICIAL DEPARTMENT BROCHURE!

(ping!) You have new mail!

EnlaRge YouR THeS1s!
MAke y0Ur ADvisor Happier!
HOT ANAlySis T00Lz!

ClicK HEre!
JORGE CHAM © 2006

what are you doing?
WHAT! ME? NOTHING! I CLICKED BY ACCIDENT!

PROF. SMITH!!
HAVE YOU SEEN HIM??

HE'S SUPPOSED TO BE AT MY THESIS DEFENSE, BUT NOBODY KNOWS WHERE HE IS!!
AAAAHH!!

hmm. i have the nagging feeling i'm supposed to be somewhere right now.
JORGE CHAM © 2006

eh. how important can it be?
THE DAILY COURTER

CECILIA?
BAM!
JORGE CHAM © 2006

NAPPING?
HIDING.

HERE, I MADE COMMENTS ON THE PAPER YOU WROTE.

UM...
I GOT A LITTLE CARRIED AWAY WITH THE RED INK...

SO I SUMMARIZED MY COMMENTS IN THE BACK PAGE.
RE-WRITE
JORGE CHAM © 2006

IS... IS THERE ANYTHING YOU LIKED ABOUT IT?
IT DIDN'T MAKE ME VOMIT.

SO, ANY PLANS FOR FRIDAY NIGHT?
OH, I HAVE PLANS.
BIG PLANS.
JORGE CHAM © 2006

FRIDAY NIGHT:
PLANS TO GET OUT OF THIS PLACE SOME DAY.

RIIIIING...

uh, hello?
CECILIA! YOU'RE STILL IN THE LAB!? IT'S FRIDAY NIGHT!

what could possibly be so important!?
um...
JORGE CHAM © 2006

YOU MEAN BESIDES MY CAREER, MY FUTURE AND MY LIFE?
what life?
(bing!) new mail from Prof. Jones...

CECILIA, IT'S FRIDAY NIGHT! WHY ARE YOU STILL IN THE LAB?
are you kidding? this is the best time to work!

NO DISTRACTIONS, IT'S QUIET, I HAVE ALL THE SERVERS TO MYSELF...

CONDITIONS ARE PERFECT FOR OPTIMAL PRODUCTIVITY!
JORGE CHAM © 2006

YOU'RE JUST SURFING THE WEB, AREN'T YOU?
yeah, my motiva-tion couldn't care less about optimal conditions.

C'MON!
I CAN'T!
BUT IT'S FRIDAY NIGHT!
SO?

WHO SAID YOU'RE SUPPOSED TO GO OUT ON FRIDAY NIGHTS, ANYWAY?
you're hopeless. talk to you later.

JORGE CHAM © 2006

HEY! THERE'S HOPE FOR YOU YET!
ACTUALLY, THE SERVER CRASHED.

ALLRIGHT, LET'S SEE...
BABY FORMULA...

DIAPERS...

RAMEN...
JORGE CHAM © 2006

THIS SHOULD LAST US WHAT, A COUPLE OF DAYS?
ra mum!

UH, SO THEN THIS WEEK I RECALIBRATED THE SCANNER AND BLAH BLAH BLAH...
ZZZZ

...IT TOOK ME DAYS TO PROCESS THE RESULTS, BUT BLAH BLAH...
ZZZZ

...AND SO THE DATA SHOWS THAT...
NO NO, THAT'S UNACCEPTABLE! REDO THE EXPERIMENTS!
JORGE CHAM © 2006

I... but... yes, sir.
ZZZ

CHECK IT OUT, WE WENT UP A NOTCH IN THE GRAD SCHOOL RANKINGS!
NO WAY!

HIGH FIVE!
YES!
ALLRIGHT!
WHOO!

yeah...
JORGE CHAM © 2006

THINK WE HAD ANYTHING TO DO WITH IT?
IF IT WERE UP TO US, WE'D PROBABLY GET THE WHOLE SCHOOL DIS-QUALIFIED.

RRRRIIIIIIIING...
RRRRIIIIIIIING...

RRRRIIIIIIIING...
RRRRIIIIIIIING...

RRRRIIIIII
AARRHH! **I'LL** GET IT, YOU LAZY BASTARDS!!
JORGE CHAM © 2006

YEAH RIGHT. LIKE **HE** WAS BEING PRO-DUCTIVE.
we have a phone?

HMM, NOT VERY CROWDED HERE TODAY. PEOPLE MUST BE RUSHING TO FILE THEIR TAXES.

I DON'T KNOW WHY THEY WAIT 'TILL THE LAST MINUTE.
I FILED MINE THE FIRST WEEK OF JANUARY.

JORGE CHAM © 2006

TAXES ARE DUE THIS WEEK??
Yessir, there's nothing like counting how little you make a year to motivate you to work.

HERE ARE YOUR DRINKS. CAN I SEE SOME I.D.?
YOU'RE GOING TO CARD US?

HOW OLD DO YOU THINK WE ARE??
WE MAY STILL BE STUDENTS, BUT WE'RE NOT KIDS! GRAD STUDENTS ARE ADULTS TOO!

UH...
JORGE CHAM © 2006

...SORRY, I DIDN'T SEE THE "BITTER GRAD STUDENT" SIGN ON YOUR FOREHEAD.
CECILIA, YOU ORDERED WATER!
well, yeah, that's all i can afford.

The Lab Food Chain
A Delicate and Balanced Ego-system
Funding Program Manager
Faculty
Post-Doc
PhD student
Master's Student
Undergrad
JORGE CHAM © 2006

SO YOU SEE, UNDERGRADS, IT'S ALL PART OF THE NATURAL ORDER OF THINGS.
US DOING YOUR DIRTY WORK IS NATURAL!?
I finished your taxes, Mr. Grad Student.
MOLD SAMPLES

YES, GRAD STUDENTS MAY BE LOW ON THE FOOD CHAIN, BUT YOU UNDERGRADS ARE AT THE BOTTOM.
AND THERE'S NOTHING YOU CAN DO ABOUT IT!.

WE CAN TELL PROF. JENKINS WHAT YOU GUYS DO EVERY FRIDAY NIGHT WITH THE LAB PROJECTOR.
HAZMAT

WHY CAN'T YOU JUST EXPLAIN TO US WHAT YOU'RE DOING AND LET US HELP?
OH, IT WOULD TAKE, UM... WAY TOO LONG TO GO OVER ALL THE COMPLEXITIES AND UH...
JORGE CHAM © 2006

YOU HAVE NO IDEA WHAT YOU'RE DOING, DO YOU?
IF I DID, YOU THINK I'D STILL BE HERE?
does anyone?

WELL, THIS FOOD CHAIN STINKS! I HATE RESEARCH!
EXCUSE US?

WE'RE THE NEW HIGH SCHOOL INTERNS. WE WERE TOLD TO REPORT TO YOU?

JORGE CHAM © 2006
I COULD GET USED TO THIS.
now don't forget our laundry.

CHECK IT OUT, THAT GUY BROUGHT A TUPPERWARE TO THE SEMINAR.
NO WAY!

THE NERVE.
SHAME-LESS.
TOTALLY.

JORGE CHAM © 2006

ALTHOUGH... IT IS BETTER THAN USING OUR POCKETS.
i'm grabbing the whole tray. cover me.

...your message after the beep.
HELLO, CECILIA, IT'S MOM. I GUESS YOU MUST BE BUSY DOING, UH, WHATEVER IT IS YOU DO.

ANYWAY, I WAS JUST AT MAVIS' AND HER DAUGHTER CAME TO VISIT. SUCH A NICE AND SUCCESSFUL GIRL!
AND SUCH BEAUTIFUL CHILDREN!

SHE SAID SHE HAS A MALE CO-WORKER WHO'S SINGLE.
NOW, SCOTT IS VERY NICE, BUT YOU'RE NOT GETTING ANY YOUNGER. I HAD TWO KIDS BY THE TIME I WAS YOUR AGE!
JORGE CHAM © 2006

anyways, just calling to wish you a happy birthday. bye!
...
SEE, THIS IS WHY I DON'T EVEN OWN A PHONE.

ARE YOU SURE YOU DON'T WANT A DRINK?
ARE YOU KIDDING?

DO YOU KNOW WHAT I CAN BUY FOR THE PRICE OF AN ALCO-HOLIC DRINK?
I RATHER SPEND MY MONEY ON IMPORTANT THINGS.

another water, please.
JORGE CHAM © 2006

HOW MUCH **IS** A BAR OF CHOCO-LATE THESE DAYS?
the high-end single origin 70% dark cacao? about 50 packs of ramen.

HEY, THERE'S SCOTT!
OH MAN, HE'S NEVER GOING TO FIND US IN THIS CROWD.
scott?
JORGE CHAM © 2006

SCOTT! HEY!
OVER HERE!
i feel i haven't seen him in years ...

SO, HOW WAS YOUR DAY?
OH, YOU DON'T REALLY WANT TO KNOW.

NO, TELL ME, I WANT TO KNOW MORE ABOUT WHAT YOU DO.
REALLY? WELL...

TODAY I FOUND OUT THAT THE PROBLEM I'VE BEEN WORKING ON (INTERSYMBOL INTERFERENCE OPTIMIZATION) SHOULD BE FORMULATED AS A MAX WEIGHTED RATE SUM FREQUENCY PARTITIONING TO REDUCE COMPUTATIONAL COMPLEXITY.
JORGE CHAM © 2006

UM... IS THAT A GOOD THING OR A BAD THING?
I'M NOT SURE. CAN WE STOP BY THE LAB ON THE WAY HOME?

I'LL JUST BE A MINUTE...
GOSH, CECILIA, HOW DO YOU FIND ANYTHING IN THIS MESS?

OH, I KNOW IT LOOKS CHAOTIC, BUT IT'S ALL CAREFULLY ORGANIZED IN AN INTRICATE PILE SYSTEM.

THAT'S MY RESEARCH PAPERS PILE, MY CLASS STUFF PILE, MY BANK STUFF PILE...
JORGE CHAM © 2006

WHAT'S THIS PILE?
THE "I DON'T KNOW WHICH PILE TO PUT IT IN" PILE.

I ALWAYS IMAGINED A RESEARCH LAB TO BE A STRANGE AND EXCITING PLACE.
WANT ME TO GIVE YOU THE "GRAND TOUR"?

THAT'S THE WATER FOUNTAIN.
...THAT'S THE COFFEE MACHINE.

THIS IS THE COPIER ROOM AND...
...OVER THERE ARE THE REST-ROOMS.
JORGE CHAM © 2006

THAT'S IT?
DISAPPOINTED?
SO WAS I.

WRITING YOUR THESIS OUTLINE

NOTHING SAYS "I'M ALMOST DONE" TO YOUR ADVISOR/ SPOUSE/PARENTS LIKE PRETENDING YOU HAVE A PLAN

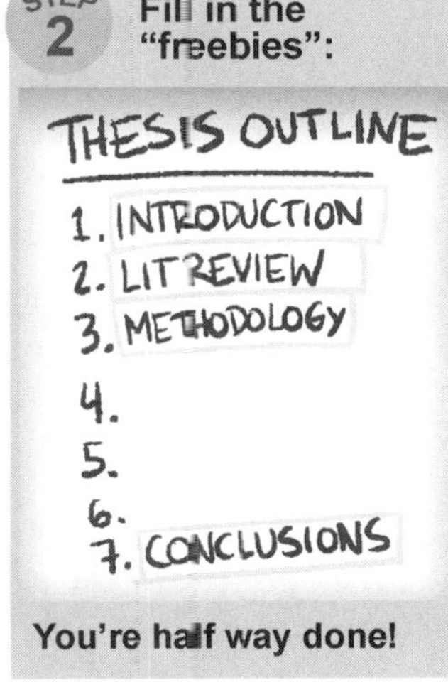

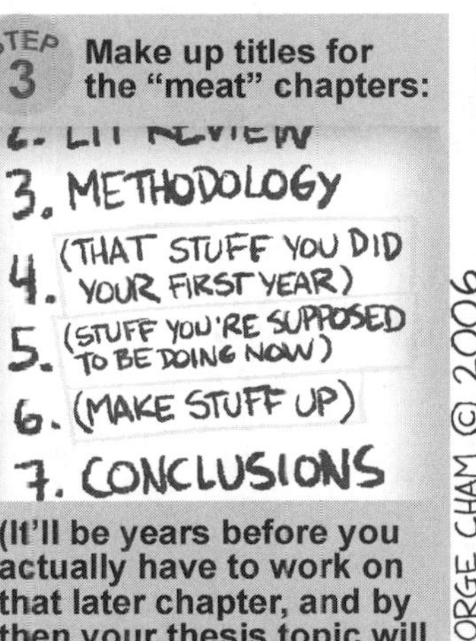

YOU'RE MOVING TO LONDON!?
whoa, hey...

SLOW DOWN, CECILIA...
IT'S JUST A JOB OFFER. LET'S NOT OVER-REACT.

JORGE CHAM © 2006

BEANS!
WITH TOAST!
FOR BREAK-FAST!!
ok, new plan.

I SHOULD JUST TURN THEM DOWN.
NO, WAIT.

IT'S NOT FAIR THAT YOU PUT YOUR CAREER ON HOLD LIKE THAT.
YOU SHOULD TAKE THE JOB.

WE WOULDN'T BE APART THAT LONG ANYWAY.
I SHOULD BE FINISHED BY NEXT YEAR.
REALLY?
JORGE CHAM © 2006

BUT THAT'S WHAT YOU SAID LAST YEAR.
WAS IT?
AND THE YEAR BEFORE.
ok, new plan.

YOUR THESIS TITLE
CONDENSING OVER HALF A DECADE OF YOUR LIFE IN ONE SENTENCE.

www.phdcomics.com

the colon
Can't decide what to title your thesis? Use a colon!

a preposition
A good preposition tells your readers "hey, this is not just a futile exercise"

"Witty catch-phrase" : Length-enhanced superlative verbiage with prolixity in/of/for Obscure topic few people care about.

witty catchphrase
Makes people think you're hip and culturally relevant. Only marginally related to the actual thesis? No problem.

the boring stuff
Nothing says "academic rigor" like a long string of dry scientific-sounding terminology and fancy buzzwords.

obscure topic few people care about
Sad, but true.

yaaawn.
zzzz
COMIX

CLOMP CLOMP CLOMP

type type type type type ty
JORGE CHAM © 2006

GRAD SCHOOL SURVIVAL TIP #98: LEARN TO RECOGNIZE YOUR ADVISOR'S FOOTSTEPS.
is he gone?
zzzz

OH. HEY.
SOMEBODY CALLED FOR YOU.
REALLY?

YEAH, IT SOUNDED REALLY URGENT.
WHO WAS IT??

IT WAS, UM...
SOMEONE CALLED BILL.
OR MARY. I'M NOT SURE.
or was it bob?
JORGE CHAM © 2006

GREAT. WHEN DID THEY CALL?
LAST WEEK. WHEN YOU WENT TO THE BATHROOM.

MIKE! WHAT ARE YOU DOING??

JORGE CHAM © 2006

UH, WORKING?
I KNOW! YOU'RE FREAKING US OUT!
what's the world come to?

SORRY I'M LATE, I...
WHERE IS EVERY-BODY?
AREN'T WE HAVING A MEETING?

UH, THEY'RE ALL OUT SICK, SIR...
JORGE CHAM © 2006

"...IT'S THE FEVER."

DEPARTU
CHCONT
JORGE CHAM © 2006

DO YOU THINK WE'LL BE OK?
OH SURE. ALMOST EVERYONE I KNOW HAS DONE THE LONG DISTANCE THING.

AND THEY SURVIVED?
ACTUALLY, THEY ALL BROKE UP.
but we're different.

WE'LL SEE EACH OTHER SOON, RIGHT?
UH, CLASSES DON'T END FOR ANOTHER TWO MONTHS ...

I THOUGHT YOU WEREN'T TAKING ANY CLASSES.
SCOTT, JUST BECAUSE I HAVE A FLEXIBLE SCHEDULE, I CAN DO ALL MY WORK FROM MY LAPTOP...

..AND NOBODY CARES IF I COME INTO THE LAB OR NOT, DOESN'T MEAN I CAN JUST... TAKE OFF WHENEVER I WANT!
JORGE CHAM © 2006

...DOES IT?
hey, a virtual salary deserves a virtual employee.

I'LL CALL YOU WHEN I GET THERE.
OK. OR JUST TEXT MESSAGE ME.

OR EMAIL ME.
OR INSTANT MESSAGE ME.
OR SKYPE ME.
JORGE CHAM © 2006

IF ONLY IT WEREN'T SO CONVENIENT TO BE APART THESE DAYS.
ACTUALLY, JUST HUG ME.

UH OH, WHAT'S WRONG?

I'VE NO IDEA WHAT TO DO NEXT FOR MY RESEARCH.
IF I ASK PROF. SMITH FOR HELP, HE'LL THINK I'M AN IDIOT!

BUT IF DON'T ASK HIM FOR HELP, HE'LL THINK I'VE BEEN SLACKING OFF ALL WEEK!
JORGE CHAM © 2006

SO WHAT ARE YOU GOING TO DO?
AVOID HIM ALTOGETHER. HOPEFULLY HE'LL FORGET I EXIST.

ABOUT YOUR LATEST DRAFT, TAJEL...
YES..?

IT'S TOO SHORT.

TOO SHORT?
BUT LAST WEEK YOU SAID IT WAS TOO LONG!
JORGE CHAM © 2006

WAIT A MINUTE... DID YOU EVEN READ IT??
AS A RULE, I ONLY READ THE SECOND TO LAST DRAFT.

2AM. REPORT DUE IN A FEW HOURS.
TIME TO BRING OUT THE OL' WHIZ KID MAGIC.

CRANK IT OUT LAST MINUTE, JUST LIKE THE OLD DAYS.
I CAN DO THIS.

BUT FIRST I'LL CHECK EMAIL.
ooh, what's this?
JORGE CHAM © 2006

ZZZZZZ...

YES!
I DID IT!
IT WORKS!!

I ACTUALLY GOT IT TO WORK!
THAT IS SO AWESOME!!
I CAN'T BELIEVE IT!

OH, MAN...
ALL THE PAIN AND SUFFERING... IT'S MOMENTS LIKE THESE THAT MAKE IT ALL WORTH IT!
JORGE CHAM © 2006

...FOR ABOUT TWO SECONDS.
there's a typo in your calculations.

HMM.
I FEEL A LITTLE... OFF TODAY.

I NEED TO BE REMINDED HOW BRILLIANT I AM.
JORGE CHAM © 2006

JUDY, SEND IN ONE OF MY POST-DOCS.

<New Mail from Prof. Smith:>
To all lab members:
I'll be out of the office for the next two weeks (family vacation).
SAMPLES

I'm bringing my laptop and will be checking e-mail several times a day. I'll be expecting updates from all of you on the status of your projects.
JORGE CHAM © 2006

Any urgent matters of research, you can reach me at...

HEY, SO... PROF. SMITH IS OUT OF TOWN. ARE WE STILL HAVING A MEETING?

WHAT?

WELL, LET'S SEE, WHY DON'T WE ASK THE SENIOR MEMBER OF THE LAB.
MIKE?
ZZZZZ...
JORGE CHAM © 2006

ALL IN AGREEMENT, SAY "AYE"
AYE
AYE
b-but... i made handouts!

LAB HAZARD RATING SYSTEM

Post this rating system to allow visitors and potential members to quickly and easily identify risks posed by exposure or prolonged contact to a particular research group.

Health Hazard

4 - Major emotional/career injury likely.
3 - Temporary incapacitation of productivity.
2 - Chronic exposure causes minor residual psychological damage.
1 - May experience irritation.
0 - No hazard beyond pre-existing self-esteem issues.

Air conditioning Hazard

4 - Near-hell conditions.
3 - Unbearably hot.
2 - Risk of spontaneous combustion.
1 - Moderate heat/risk of vaporization.
0 - A/C out of control. Risk of sub-zero temperatures and frost-bite.

4

1 0

BIO

Specific Hazards

"BIO" - Smelly co-worker(s)
"COR" - Corrosive cut-throat/back-stabbing reactions may occur.
"BLM" - Bitter lab manager
"VOR" - High risk of Vortex of Procrastination formation.
"PHD" - Members incessantly forward unamusing online comic strips.

Advisor Reactivity

4 - May detonate.
3 - Readily capable of explosive decomposition.
2 - Undergoes changes at elevated pressures.
1 - Somewhat stable under normal disappointment conditions.
0 - Doesn't really care about you.

DADDY... WE'RE BORED!!
i brought them into this world, i have to entertain them too?

OK, KIDS, TAKE THESE BIG RED INK MARKERS AND SCRIBBLE ALL OVER THESE PAPERS THAT DADDY'S GRAD STUDENTS MADE.
JORGE CHAM © 2006

WHAT?
IT'S NOT EXPLOITATION IF THEY'RE LEARNING SOMETHING...

HEY, MIKE...
WE'VE ALL BEEN WONDERING... WHY ARE YOU STILL HERE?

WELL, I WAS GOING TO GO HOME, BUT THERE'S A SEMINAR AT 4:00pm I REALLY WANT TO CHECK OUT.
JORGE CHAM © 2006

NO, I MEAN, WHY DO YOU STILL COME TO THE LAB?
DIDN'T YOU DEFEND A WHILE AGO?
word on the street is they're going to have mini-pizzas.
they're like regular pizzas, but small.

SO YOU DEFENDED, BUT YOU HAVEN'T FINISHED WRITING YOUR THESIS?
YEAH, IT'S MY COMMITTEE

THEY'RE BEING REALLY PICKY ABOUT MY EXPERI-MENTAL VALIDATION RESULTS.
JORGE CHAM © 2006

WHAT'S WRONG WITH THEM?
I DON'T HAVE ANY.
since when do *they* care about "reality"?

THE CONFERENCE CALL:
CAN YOU HEAR ME NOW?
YES, PROF. SMITH.
OK, YOU WERE SAYING?

I SAID I PRO-CESSED THE...
WAIT, I CAN'T HEAR-
I PRO-CESSED THE...
NO, I STILL CAN'T-
THE DATA! I PRO-
JORGE CHAM © 2006

HOLD ON, I GOT-
HONEY, DO YOU HAVE TO WORK-
DAD! JUNIOR WON'T LET ME-
WAAAH!!
I'M ON THE PHONE!
Z Z Z

CECILIA, HAVE YOU-
WAIT WAIT! I'M ALMOST DONE WITH THIS BOOK!

JORGE CHAM © 2006

THE RESULTS WERE INCONCLUSIVE!? WHAT A GYP!
IT'S A RESEARCH BOOK!?

I DON'T KNOW, PROF. RIVERA...
LATELY I FEEL LIKE IT'S ALL GOING IN THE WRONG DIRECTION.

IT'S... IT'S LIKE THE FACTS SAY ONE THING, BUT ALL THE CONCLUSIONS SAY SOMETHING ELSE. IT JUST DOESN'T MAKE SENSE!

YOU'D THINK BY NOW THINGS WOULD BE CLEAR, BUT IT JUST KEEPS GETTING WORSE AND WORSE...
JORGE CHAM © 2006

ARE WE STILL TALKING ABOUT YOUR THESIS?
THE WORLD, PROF. RIVERA. THE WORLD.

UH OH.
WHAT ARE YOU LIBERAL HIPPIES PROTESTING NOW?

IS IT THE SENSELESS KILLING IN THE MIDDLE EAST? GLOBAL WARMING? GOVERNMENT WIRETAPPING? THE GROWING UNION OF CHURCH AND STATE?

STOP
JORGE CHAM © 2006

YES.
ACTUALLY, I'M WITH YOU.
you got another sign?

WHO'D HAVE THOUGHT. A GUY WITH A BOW-TIE AND A VEGAN ACTUALLY AGREEING ON SOMETHING.
WEIRD, HUH?

IT'S LIKE, HOW MUCH LONGER ARE PEOPLE GOING TO LET THIS ADMINISTRATION CONTINUE ACTING SO IRRESPONSIBLY?
I KNOW...
JORGE CHAM © 2006

YOU MEAN THE BUDGET DEFICIT, RIGHT?
THE BUDGET WHAT?

WELL, IT WAS INTERESTING TALKING WITH YOU.
YOU'RE IN THE ECON DEPART-MENT?
YEAH...

MY RESEARCH IS ON GLOBALIZATION AND HOW IT'S AN AWESOME THING FOR COMMERCE AND CORPORATE EXPANSION.

JORGE CHAM © 2006

WELL, SEE YOU NEVER.
ENJOY YOUR GRANOLA.

DADDY, WHY ARE STARFISH SHAPED LIKE STARS?
UH...

THAT'S A VERY INTER-ESTING QUESTION, SADIE. FUNCTIONAL ADAPTABIL-ITY AND ANATOMICAL DETERMINATION IN BIO-LOGICAL SYSTEMS IS A FASCINATING ISSUE THAT CERTAINLY WARRANTS FURTHER INVESTIGATION.
JORGE CHAM © 2006

DOES THAT MEAN YOU DON'T KNOW?
IT'S BEYOND THE SCOPE OF MY RESEARCH.

AUTHOR BIOGRAPHIES:

cher complexities
ization," IEEE Trans.
oracle inequalities
Biomed. Eng., vol. 49, pp 796-804, 2002.

Author 1 is the Arthur C. and Caroline J. McCallister Distinguished Chair Professor and Anderson Faculty Scholar and the Director of the Center for Computational Research and the Natl. Inst. of Dynamical Physics. He is the recipient of the Alexander von Humboldt Prize of the Federal Republic of the Netherlands, the NSF Presidential Investigator Award, the Exceptional Achievement Medal from the Intl. Society of Engineers, the Pi Gamma Tau Industry Excellence Professorship, the Natl. Medal of Engineering, and the Medal of Honor from the Royal Academy of Scientists. He serves on the Editorial Board of the Journal of Advanced Dynamics, the Journal of Nano-Particle Computation, Physik-Publikation and several other journals and on the Advisory Board of multiple industry consortiums. He holds Honorary Doctorates from the Universidad Politecnica de Madrid, Tsing-Chua Beijing University and the Universidade de Sao Paulo among others. He has
too numerous to mention here.

simple GCV
smoothing," Biometrika, vol. 88, pp. 11

Author 2 is a grad student.

Dynamics, Vol. 54, No. 8, Augu

ISN'T THIS NICE?

GETTING AWAY FROM IT ALL, SPENDING QUALITY TIME WITH OUR FAMILY...
WHAT A BEAUTIFUL MOMENT.

JORGE CHAM © 2006

YOU'RE THINKING ABOUT RESEARCH AREN'T YOU?

JORGE CHAM © 2006

AAH..!

JORGE CHAM © 2006

SUMMER'S OVER ALREADY!?
WHAT HAVE I BEEN DOING FOR THREE MONTHS??

surf surf...
JORGE CHAM © 2006

OH.
right.

UH, HI. WE'RE NEW MASTER'S STUDENTS.
IS THIS PROF. SMITH'S RE-SEARCH GROUP MEETING?

ACTUALLY, YOU WANNA GO OUT THE DOOR, TAKE A RIGHT, AND JUST KEEP GOING.
OH. UH... THANKS.
JORGE CHAM © 2006

IT'S FOR THEIR OWN GOOD.
JUST KEEP GOING AND DON'T EVER LOOK BACK!

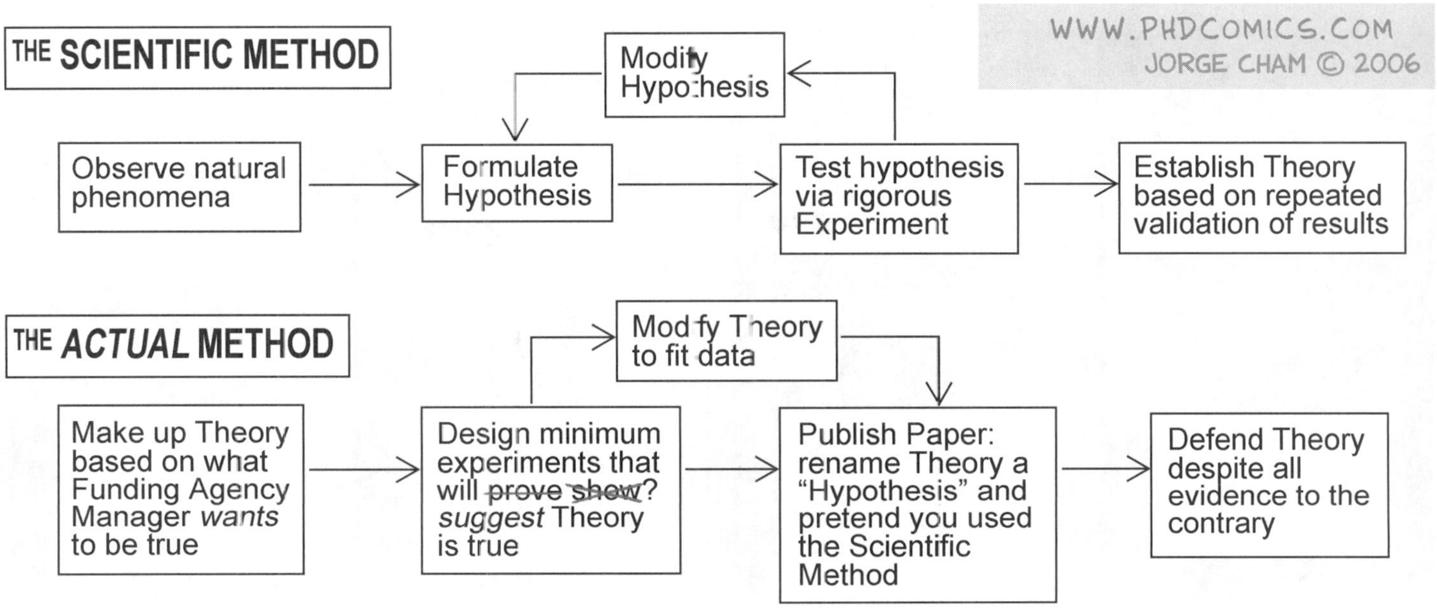

THE SCIENTIFIC METHOD

Observe natural phenomena → Formulate Hypothesis → Test hypothesis via rigorous Experiment → Establish Theory based on repeated validation of results

Test hypothesis via rigorous Experiment → Modify Hypothesis → Formulate Hypothesis

THE *ACTUAL* METHOD

Make up Theory based on what Funding Agency Manager *wants* to be true → Design minimum experiments that will ~~prove~~ ~~show~~? *suggest* Theory is true → Publish Paper: rename Theory a "Hypothesis" and pretend you used the Scientific Method → Defend Theory despite all evidence to the contrary

Design minimum experiments → Modify Theory to fit data → Publish Paper

LAB
JORGE CHAM © 2006

UNDERGRAD COOTIES! EEWWW!

JORGE CHAM © 2006

THE "CARRYING PAPERS AROUND SO YOU FEEL PRODUCTIVE" PHASE.
DUDE, THAT'S TOO FAR.
WHAT?
FLUSH!

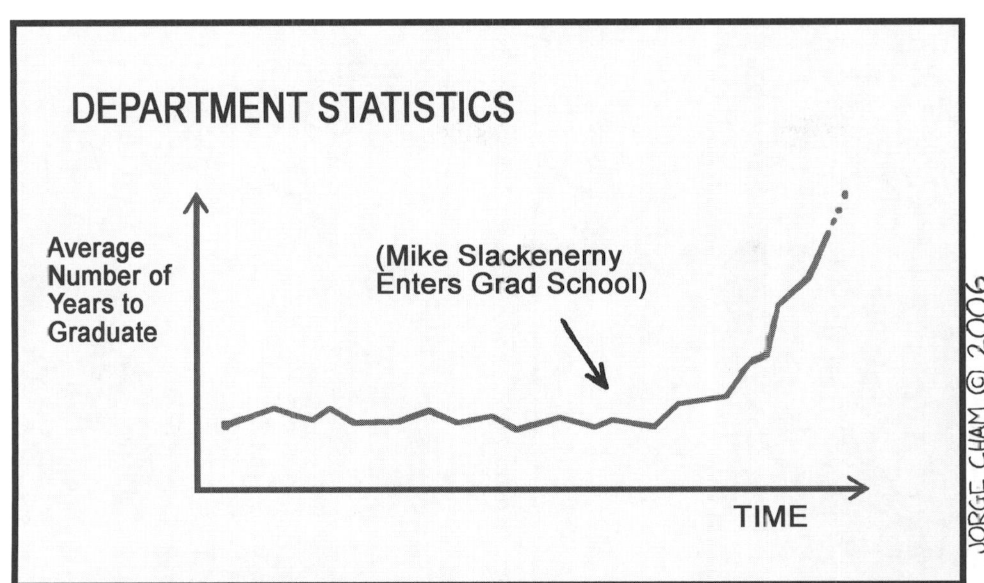
DEPARTMENT STATISTICS
Average Number of Years to Graduate
(Mike Slackenerny Enters Grad School)
TIME

JORGE CHAM © 2006
MIKE, WE NEED TO TALK.

MIKE, I'LL BE FRANK.
YOUR TAKING SO LONG TO GRADUATE DOES NOT REFLECT WELL ON ME.

THE ONLY REASON I HAVEN'T CUT YOU OFF IS THAT I BELIEVE IN A PROFESSOR'S COMMITMENT TO SEEING THEIR STUDENTS FINISH, NO MATTER HOW LONG IT TAKES.

PROF. SMITH... I... I DON'T KNOW WHAT TO SAY.
JORGE CHAM © 2006

I ALWAYS THOUGHT IT WAS BECAUSE I'M THE ONLY ONE WHO KNOWS HOW TO USE OUR ARCANE LAB EQUIPMENT.
WELL, THAT TOO.

MIKE, I WANT YOU TO TEACH OTHERS HOW TO USE THE LAB EQUIPMENT.
JUST IN CASE.
IN CASE WHAT?

I ACTUALLY GRADUATE?
GET HIT BY A TRUCK.
JORGE CHAM © 2006

I'M GOING TO MISS OUR LITTLE CHATS.
JUST LOOK BEFORE YOU CROSS.

SLUUURP!!

SLUUUURP!!

SLUUUURP!!
JORGE CHAM © 2006

WHAT?

PREVIOUSLY, ON
LOST
ONE TICKET TO GRAD SCHOOL, PLEASE.
HAVE A NICE TRIP.
WHAT... WHAT HAPPENED??
RUN! QUALS!
AAAHH! MY EGO!
I FEEL LIKE WE'RE BEING WATCHED...
JUST PUSH THE BUTTON!
DARPA
>:1.57079632678
WHY!?
WHY ARE WE HERE??
OOH, RAMEN!
DARPA
NACHOS
COFFEE
DARPA PIZZA

OK, BEFORE I PASS ON MY KNOWLEDGE OF THIS LAB EQUIPMENT, I FEEL I SHOULD WARN YOU.
WHAT?

KNOWING HOW TO USE IT WILL MAKE YOU MORE INDISPENSABLE TO THE LAB...

BUT IT WILL ALSO MAKE EVERYONE COME TO YOU TO HELP THEM WITH THEIR RESEARCH.
JORGE CHAM © 2006

ON SECOND THOUGHT, I THINK I'LL...
TOO LATE. WELCOME TO MY NIGHTMARE.

ALLRIGHT, SO HOW DOES IT WORK?
WELL FIRST, YOU FLIP IT ON...

KLUNK KLUNK KLUNK KLUNK
IS THAT NOR-
QUIETER THAN USUAL...

KLUNK!
JORGE CHAM © 2006

I ALWAYS WANTED TO WORK WITH CUTTING EDGE TECHNOLOGY.
ZZ ZZ
IT WAS CUTTING EDGE WHEN I STARTED.

I DON'T GET IT.
THEY HAVE MACHINES THAT CAN DO THIS TEN TIMES FASTER NOW.
WHY DON'T WE JUST BUY A NEW ONE?

COST-BENEFIT ANALYSIS
New!
DATA MASTER™ 3000
$$
Grad Student Time
¢
HMM...
JORGE CHAM © 2006

OH.
WHEN THEY SAY "COST-BENEFIT", THEY DON'T USUALLY MEAN OUR BENEFIT.
HERE, PROCESS THIS.

ALLRIGHT, I PULLED THE LEVER AND PUSHED THE BUTTON.
SO WHAT'S THE BIG SECRET TO GETTING THIS TO WORK?

AN INTRICATE CALIBRATION ROUTINE?
A COMPLICATED WAY OF CONNECTING THINGS?
A SPECIAL PROGRAMMING HACK?

BAM!
JORGE CHAM © 2006

THAT'S IT!?
IT TOOK ME MOST OF THE 1990'S TO FIGURE THAT ONE OUT.
PURRRR...

LIKE I SAID, BEING THE "GO TO" GUY FOR A LAB MACHINE HAS ITS DRAWBACKS. YOUR ONLY HOPE:
CULTIVATE AN AIR OF UNHELPFULNESS.

YOU DON'T WANT TO BE OUTRIGHT UNHELP-FUL. YOU JUST WANT PEOPLE TO THINK TWICE BEFORE ASKING YOU FOR HELP.
HOW DO I DO THAT?

GRAAH! CAN'T YOU FIGURE ANYTHING OUT BY YOURSELF!?
FINE! I'LL TELL YOU HOW TO DO IT! YEESH!!!
S-SORRY! I, I...
JORGE CHAM © 2006

OH...
IF YOU WORK HARD, SOON NO ONE WILL EVEN WANT TO TALK TO YOU.

WELL, I'VE TAUGHT YOU EVERYTHING I KNOW ABOUT THIS LAB MACHINE. YOU ARE NOW THE RESIDENT EXPERT.

HERE IS YOUR IMMUNITY IDOL.

...AND YOUR NEW BADGE OF OFFICE.
SLAP!
JORGE CHAM © 2006

UH, EXCUSE ME?
ENJOY BEING IMPORTANT.

ANYTHING INTERESTING IN THE SCHOOL NEWSPAPER?
OH, HEY, TAJEL.

UH, LET'S SEE...
PROFILES OF THE UNDER-GRAD ELECTIONS... DEBATE OVER THE UNDERGRADS' ACTIVITY FEES BUDGET...
...AND THE UNDERGRAD PROTESTS TO BRING BACK TATER-TOTS TO THE CAFETERIA MENU.
THE DAILY TECH
JORGE CHAM © 2006

SO... NO.
I'M EATING BY MYSELF. AT LEAST IT'S NOT A RESEARCH PAPER.

ALLRIGHT... EATING BY MYSELF.
IT'S COOL.

NO REASON TO FEEL SELF-CONSCIOUS...
I'M SURE NOBODY IS LOOKING AT ME...
JUDGING ME...

JORGE CHAM © 2006

I AM NOT A LOSER!!

AH, WHO CARES WHAT OTHER PEOPLE THINK.
THERE'S NOTHING WRONG WITH EATING ALONE...

I HAVE NOTHING TO PROVE.
I GOT PLENTY OF FRIENDS!
JORGE CHAM © 2006

...online.

KRAKOOM!
AAARGH!

WHERE ARE THE REFERENCES I ASKED FOR??
COMING MASTER!

LONG HAVE I TOILED TO CREATE A CREATURE WORTHY OF MY NAME... OF CARRYING MY RECOMMENDATION FOR FACULTY POSITIONS!
AND NOW AT LAST...
JORGE CHAM © 2006

BEHOLD...
MY LEGACY!!
KRAKOOM!

THROUGH MY GENIUS, I WILL TRANSFORM THIS LIFELESS MASS INTO A BEING OF PURE ACADEMIC RIGOR!
THEY WILL TREMBLE BEFORE MY NAME!

ARROGANT, THEY CALLED ME!
DRUNK ON ILLUSIONS OF GRANDEUR AND GODHOOD!
JORGE CHAM © 2006

I SAID, DUH!
I'M A PROFESSOR. OF COURSE I THINK I'M A GOD!

AND NOW, MY CREATION...
AWAKEN!!

KRAKOOM!
ZZZRRK!!!

JORGE CHAM © 2006

SO? WHY DOESN'T HE WAKE UP?
IT'S ONLY 11am. I'D WAIT AT LEAST 'TILL NOON.
ZZZZ

DAYLIGHT SAVINGS TIME: FALL BACK

I WANT YOU TO KNOW, I EXPECT ALL MY STUDENTS TO BE IN THE LAB DURING REGULAR WORKING HOURS.

YOU MEAN 9 TO 5?
I MEAN 6 am TO MIDNIGHT.

JORGE CHAM © 2006

BUT MY STIPEND ONLY COVERS 20 HOURS A WEEK.
OF QUALITY WORK, NOT GRAD STUDENT "WORK".

YOU SEE, I DON'T EXPECT MY STUDENTS TO HAVE A LIFE OUTSIDE THE LAB.
I DIDN'T, AND NEITHER SHOULD YOU.

UM, THEN WHY DID THE GRAD SCHOOL APPLICATION FORM ASK ABOUT EXTRA-CURRICULAR ACTIVITIES?
JORGE CHAM © 2006

BECAUSE I DIDN'T WRITE THE APPLICATION.
IS CRYING CONSIDERED A HOBBY?

RESEARCH SHOULD BE THE SOLE FOCUS OF YOUR LIFE.
I EXPECT YOU TO EAT, DRINK AND SLEEP RESEARCH.

I'M ALLOWED TO SLEEP?
ONLY IN A LIE-AWAKE-AT-NIGHT-OBSESSING-OVER-IT KIND OF WAY.

OUTSIDE INTERESTS ONLY TELL ME YOU'RE NOT SERIOUS ABOUT GETTING YOUR PHD.
I MEAN, WHAT COULD BE MORE INTERESTING THAN OUR RESEARCH?
JORGE CHAM © 2006

I... I CAN'T ANSWER THAT.
EXACTLY. NOTHING.

MORE
FUTILE ATTEMPTS AT HAVING A
"NORMAL LIFE"

JORGE CHAM © 2006

HEY, A COUPLE OF US ARE GOING OUT TO EAT. WANNA GO?

SORRY, I CAN'T.
I WENT OUT LAST WEEK. I CAN'T REALLY AFFORD TO DO IT AGAIN UNTIL...
JORGE CHAM © 2006

...NEXT YEAR.
WHERE'D YOU GO?
McDONALD'S.

OH, MAN, NOBODY'S MADE COFFEE YET?

grumble
grumble
I SWEAR...
COFFEE
JORGE CHAM © 2006

IT'S LIKE PEOPLE JUST WAIT FOR ME TO DO EVERYTHING AROUND HERE.

OH MAN, I FEEL WEAK...
CAN'T... SEEM TO... STAY AWAKE...

IT'S...
THIS COFFEE...
IT'S... IT'S...
IT'S DECAF!!
JORGE CHAM © 2006

NOOOOooo ...ZZZZZ
heh heh...

AAAAAHHH!!
THIS RESEARCH IS IMPOSSIBLE!!
latest journal issue.

Paper With Same Title You Were Going To Give Your Thesis
JORGE CHAM © 2006

AAAAAHHH!!
SOMEONE ALREADY DID IT!!

WELL, THANKS FOR INVITING ME TO JOIN YOUR THANKSGIVING DINNER.
OH, DIDN'T TAJEL TELL YOU?
US HUMANITIES MAJORS DON'T CELEBRATE THANKSGIVING.

THANKSGIVING IS JUST ANOTHER SHAMELESS COMMERCIALIZED TOOL OF AMERICANIZATION THAT PERPETUATES FALSE MYTHS TO HIDE A BRUTAL HISTORY OF COLONIZATION AND CULTURAL GENOCIDE.
JORGE CHAM © 2006

THEN WHAT ARE WE CELEBRATING?
NO UNDER-GRADS FOR A WEEK!
who wants some tofurkey?

AAAAAAAAAAAAAA

AAAAAAAAAAAAAA

AAAAAAAAAAAAAA
JORGE CHAM © 2006

AAAAAHHHRRRGGH!!!!
STILL AT IT?
ONE WEEK AND COUNTING.

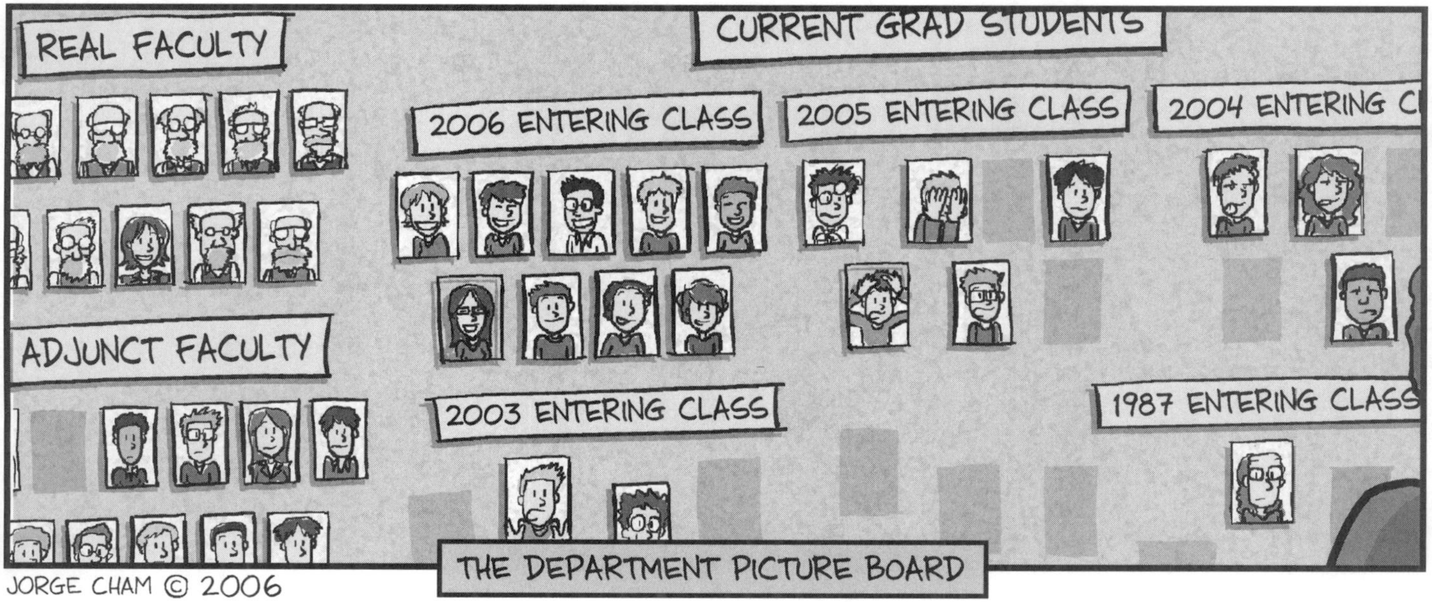

REAL FACULTY
CURRENT GRAD STUDENTS
2006 ENTERING CLASS
2005 ENTERING CLASS
2004 ENTERING C
ADJUNCT FACULTY
2003 ENTERING CLASS
1987 ENTERING CLASS
THE DEPARTMENT PICTURE BOARD

elusive, it suggests the scheme shown in Figure 12.

Conclusions

In this paper we have reviewed a framework for characterizing the issues in identifying an approximate model for contextualizing future possible exploratory directions that infer the challenges related to verifying the need for further investigation.

References

[1] Andersen, R. A., Burdick, J. W., Scherberger, H., Musallam, S., Pesaran, B., and Cham, J. G., Trends in Cognitive Science Volume 8, Issue 11, Novembe

JORGE CHAM © 2006

SO, DO THEY USE THE SAME APPROACH YOU DO?
UH, NOT QUITE...

HOW SO?
THEY USE A Σ COEFFICIENT OF 0.2.
AND YOU?
Σ = 0.23

THAT'S A HUGE DIFFERENCE.
IT IS?
AT LEAST, THAT'S HOW YOU'LL WRITE ABOUT IT IN YOUR PAPER.
JORGE CHAM © 2006

WHAT IF THEIR RESULTS ARE BETTER?
"EXPLORATION OF THE PARAMETER SPACE"

WELL, I HOPE YOU LEARNED YOUR LESSON.

THERE'S ONLY ONE WAY TO MAKE SURE NOBODY PUBLISHES RESULTS BEFORE YOU DO.
JORGE CHAM © 2006

WORK HARDER?
CHOOSE A TOPIC NOBODY CARES ABOUT.

Holiday Gift Ideas
For the Budget-Conscious Grad Student

www.phdcomics.com
JORGE CHAM © 2006

UH, SO... PROF. WILSON, ANY PLANS FOR THE HOLI-
HOW'S THAT PAPER COMING ALONG?
JORGE CHAM © 2006

HEY! YOU'RE NOT IN THIS DEPARTMENT!
awww, how cute!

i'm going home for the holidays, but i'm taking the laptop with me.

zzz

JORGE CHAM © 2006

uh...

Happy Winter Break!

ANOTHER YEAR ENDS...
A NEW ONE BEGINS.

WILL I BE AS BRILLIANT THIS YEAR AS I WAS THE YEAR BEFORE?
WILL I DAZZLE MY PEERS AND EARN THE AWE AND RESPECT OF GENERATIONS OF FUTURE RESEARCHERS, ONCE MORE?
JORGE CHAM © 2006

IT'S ALMOST TOO EASY AT THIS POINT.

I READ THE PAPER DRAFT YOU GAVE ME, TAJEL.
I MUST SAY, I'M DISAPPOINTED.

WHY DIDN'T YOU INCLUDE A DISCUSSION OF PREVIOUS WORK BY ROTH, ET AL.?
I DID, BUT YOU TOLD ME LAST WEEK TO TAKE IT OUT!

DID I?
WELL, PUT IT BACK.
ARE YOU SURE?
YES.
JORGE CHAM © 2006

NEXT WEEK:
TAKE IT OUT.
AARGH!!

In Memoriam

Momofuku Ando (1910-2007)

Pioneer, Procrastinator, Inventor of the Instant Ramen Noodle

"Peace will come to the world when all its people have enough to eat."

I CAN'T UNDERSTAND A WORD PROF. RIVERA WROTE ON MY PAPER DRAFT!

I MEAN, WHAT DOES HE MEAN BY THIS?
"DEFLATABLE URN OF SAUSAGE"...? "TEDDY BEAR AUGMENTATION, REWIRE ON FIRE SUCTION"..???

ACTUALLY, I THINK IT SAYS "DEPLORABLE USE OF LANGUAGE, TERRIBLE ARGUMENTATION, REWRITE ENTIRE SECTION"...
JORGE CHAM © 2007

GEE. THANKS.
IF YOU CAN'T STAND THE HEAT, STEP AWAY FROM THE FIRE SUCTION.

DRAFT 1
REVISE.

DRAFT 2
REVISE.
JORGE CHAM © 2007

DRAFT ∞
REVISE.

DRAFT APPROVED!
I'M SICK OF READING THIS. JUST TURN IT IN.
...

HELLO! READERS OFTEN ASK US:
Dear PHD,
Your comics describe my life so perfectly, it's scary!
Do you have hidden cameras pointing at me?
-Readers

AS A MATTER OF FACT, WE DO!
HERE AT PHD HEAD-QUARTERS, A DEDICATED STAFF CONSTANTLY MONITORS OUR EXTENSIVE NETWORK OF FIBEROPTIC CAMERAS, JUST WAITING FOR ONE OF YOU TO DO SOMETHING FUNNY! LET'S JOIN IN!
JORGE CHAM © 2007

SOMEONE'S GETTING ABUSED BY THEIR ADVISOR IN GUAM!
ZOOM IN! ZOOM IN!
SMILE! YOU'RE ON MISERY CAMERA!

To: All Students, Faculty and Staff
From: Office of the President

Due to severe weather conditions, classes have been cancelled for today.
JORGE CHAM © 2007

All Faculty and Staff offices will remain closed until further notice.

Grad students, of course, are still expected to work.
-The Administration

ALLRIGHT, MADE IT IN BRIGHT AND EARLY TODAY.

OH, HEY, GOOD MORNING PROF. SMITH!
SCORE!
JORGE CHAM © 2007

AWESOME. I'LL JUST SURF THE WEB A LITTLE BEFORE...

LUNCH?
WHAT? ALREADY!?

CLANG CLANG CLANG CLANG
UGH, ANOTHER FIRE ALARM DRILL!

ANG CLANG CLANG CLANG
...OR IS IT??
JORGE CHAM © 2007

CLANG CLANG CLANG CL...
must.. save... data...
YOU'D BE SO DEAD BY NOW.

THERE'S ONLY ONE CHOCOLATE CHIP COOKIE LEFT IN THE FREE FOOD LINE!

HEY! NO CUTTING!
THIS COOKIE IS MINE!
JORGE CHAM © 2007

NEVER MIND. IT'S RAISIN.
i'll take it.

I HAVE DECIDED I AM NO LONGER INTERESTED IN YOUR RESEARCH PROJECT.

UNFORTUNATELY, YOU JUMPED IN AT THE TAIL END OF ACADEMIC AND FUNDING INTEREST ON THE TOPIC.
JORGE CHAM © 2007

HOWEVER, AS MUCH AS IT BORES ME, I WILL CONTINUE TO PRETEND TO CARE THAT YOU GRADUATE.

"CONTINUE" TO PRETEND?
IT'S THE LEAST I CAN DO.

JORGE CHAM © 2007

JORGE CHAM © 2007

YOUR ADVISOR'S NEGATION FIELD

A Professor's Negation Field is the unexplained phenomenon whereby mere spatial proximity to an experimental set-up causes all working demonstrations to fail, despite the apparent laws of Physics or how many times it worked right before he/she walked into the room.

BEWARE ALSO:

The Sphere of Death. Allowing your experiment within arm's reach of your Advisor risks the possibility of immediate destruction.

HI, COME ON IN.
THANKS, PROF. SMITH.

READY?
rdfgh.

FWWOOSH!
JORGE CHAM © 2007

CECILIA, I'VE BEEN LOOKING AT YOUR ACADEMIC C.V.
YOU HAVE?

I NOTICED YOU'VE NEVER T.A.'d A CLASS BEFORE.
HOW WOULD YOU LIKE TO T.A. FOR ME THIS QUARTER?
JORGE CHAM © 2007

IT'LL BE GOOD TO SHOW SOME TEACHING EXPERIENCE WHEN YOU APPLY FOR FACULTY POSITIONS.

YOU MEAN THEY ACTUALLY CARE ABOUT TEACHING?
NO, NOT REALLY.
BUT I DO NEED SOMEONE TO COVER MY LECTURES.

Valentine's Gift ideas

For the most important person in your life... Your Advisor

Heart candy assortment

PASS ME
FUND ME
I ♥ DATA
RESPECT ME
BE MY MENTOR

the Annihilator™ 3000 red mark-up pen

Antacids and Ego Boost audio greeting card

PEPTO BISMOL
TUMS
Brilliant! Genius!

the Burst my Bubble™ balloon and sharp pin set

i have an idea!
my first thesis draft!
i'm graduating soon!
POP!
POP!

The Classic Coffee Mug

World's Best* Advisor

*The term "Best" is defined over the set A^n where n=1 number of professors who would take me as their student.

COULDN'T SLEEP? NERVOUS ABOUT CLASS TODAY?
IT'S NOT JUST THAT...

IT'S ALSO MY THESIS, MY RESEARCH... I'M ALSO FILLING OUT FACULTY APPLICATIONS, BUT I'M NOT EVEN SURE I WANT TO BE A PROFESSOR...
SO I'M LOOKING AT POSTDOCS JUST IN CASE, BUT AFTER THAT, WHAT?
JORGE CHAM © 2007

AND SCOTT IS COMING THIS WEEK! WHO KNOWS WHERE THAT RELATIONSHIP IS GOING?
WHO KNOWS WHERE ANYTHING IN MY LIFE IS GOING??

see you in class?
WHEN DID THINGS GET SO COMPLICATED!?

IT'S SO OVERWHELMING THE EMOTIONS THAT COME WITH THINKING ABOUT THE FUTURE...
riiing...

FEAR
EXCITEMENT
SELF-DOUBT...
hello?
JORGE CHAM © 2007

IT'S YOUR MOM. SHE WANTS TO KNOW IF SHE SHOULD BUY PLANE TICKETS TO ATTEND GRADUATION THIS YEAR, OR IF YOU'RE GONNA CONTINUE TO DISAPPOINT HER.
AND LET'S NOT FORGET GUILT.

SPARE A DIME, MISTER?

YOU POOR CHILD! TELL ME, WHAT LED YOU TO THIS HORRIBLE CONDITION?
'TIS ME FATHER, GOV'NOR...
RAMEN!
JORGE CHAM © 2007

'E NEVER FINISHED 'IS THESIS...

IT'S TIME TO END THIS.

ALLRIGHT, I'M DETERMINED TO FINISH THIS THESIS!
ALL I NEED NOW IS A...
TIME-LAPSE MONTAGE!
WORLD BEST DADDY
type type type
JORGE CHAM © 2007

PHEW! HOW AM I DOING?
IT'S ONLY BEEN TEN MINUTES.

full parameter space.
another with their results
auses a reflex reaction w
neuverability.§
CLICK.

THERE.
I'M DONE.
print print...
JORGE CHAM © 2007

WOW, YOUR THESIS...
IT'S... IT'S...

THINNER THAN I EXPECTED.
IT'S MY LIFE'S WORK!

THE TIME DIFFERENCE.
wait, are you 8 hours ahead or 8 hours behind?

THE INOPPORTUNE TIMING.
Risk Analy
New Messag
Cecilia says:
hey,hon!
Interest Ra
Calcuation
can't chat now...
JORGE CHAM © 2007

THE GUILT.

THE JOYS OF LONG-DISTANCE RELATIONSHIPS.

TE
7

HEY!
ARRIV
JORGE CHAM © 2007

YOU MUST BE EXHAUSTED FROM JETLAG!
IT'S NOT THAT BAD. IT WAS ONLY AN 18 HOUR FLI-

AN 18 HOUR WHAT?
zzz...

HEY...
HEY, YOU'RE UP!!

SO, WHAT DO YOU WANT TO DO TODAY?
OH, ANYTHING'S FINE. I THOUGHT YOU HAD A TON OF WORK TO DO.
JORGE CHAM © 2007

BUT YOU CAME ALL THIS WAY! AND YOU'RE ONLY HERE FOR A FEW DAYS! IT'S GOTTA BE SPECIAL! IT'S GOTTA BE PERFECT!

I MEAN, NO PRESSURE OR ANYTHING.
um, we need to talk.

DO YOU WANT TO PROOF-READ MY THESIS?
UH, SURE.

I'LL JUST...
uh...
JORGE CHAM © 2007

SNORE..!

FUNNY.
all the blood rushed out of my brain!

I FINISHED IT, PROF. SMITH.
VERY WELL. WHERE DO I SIGN?

WAIT, DON'T YOU WANT TO READ IT FIRST?
NOT REALLY.
JORGE CHAM © 2007

...UNLESS YOU WANT ME TO?
nah, i'm good.

SO, DID YOU TURN IT IN??
uh... not quite.

I'M MISSING TWO THESIS COMMITTEE MEMBER SIGNATURES. ONE OF THEM IS ON SABBATICAL IN EGYPT. THE OTHER IS ON A FIELD TRIP IN THE HIMALAYAS.
I DON'T THINK I'M GONNA MAKE THE DEADLI-
JORGE CHAM © 2007

WH- HOW-!?
just...
turn it...
...IN.
pant pant..!

MAYBE IT'S TIME WE ASKED OURSELVES WHERE WE'RE GOING WITH THIS RELATIONSHIP.
YEAH...

WE CAN'T KEEP DOING THE LONG DISTANCE THING FOREVER... IT'S TOO HARD.
JORGE CHAM © 2007

EVEN IF I GRADUATE, WHO KNOWS WHERE I'LL BE ABLE TO GET A FACULTY JOB?
PROFESSORS NEVER RETIRE! THE ONLY WAY A NEW JOB OPENS IS... IS...
IS...

...IF ONE OF THEM HAS AN UNTIMELY ACCIDENT...
let's not get too creative here.

JORGE CHAM © 2007
A Dissertation
Submitted to the
Committee
on Graduate
Studies
of

WHAT IF YOU GOT AN INDUSTRY JOB? THEN WE MIGHT HAVE A CHANCE OF ENDING UP IN THE SAME CITY.
YOU MEAN... A REAL JOB??

BUT THEN... WHAT HAVE I BEEN WORKING TOWARDS ALL THIS TIME IF NOT TO BE A PRO-FESSOR?
JORGE CHAM © 2007

I CAN'T WORK FOR "THE MAN"!
I CAN'T BE A SELL-OUT LIKE... LIKE...

LIKE ME?
LIKE A NORMAL PERSON!

Tue, Thu,
9:00am-
8:00am

Registrar's
Office
Office
of
Graduate
Studies

I GUESS IT'S NOT FAIR FOR EITHER OF US TO GIVE UP OUR CAREERS. NOT AFTER ALL WE'VE PUT INTO THEM.
YEAH...

HOW DID WE GET HERE?
I MEAN, DO I REALLY CARE THAT MUCH ABOUT MY WORK??
JORGE CHAM © 2007

MAYBE YOU DON'T. BUT I KNOW THAT IF YOU DON'T FOLLOW YOUR DREAM, YOU'RE NOT GOING TO BE HAPPY, EVEN IF YOU'RE WITH ME.

STUPID DREAM. I'M TIRED OF FOLLOWING IT.
can't you just find out where it's going?

REGISTRAR
SUBMIT YOUR THESIS HERE

REGISTRAR
SUBMIT YOUR THESIS HERE
SUBMIT!
JORGE CHAM © 2007

HOORAY!!
REGISTRAR
SUBMIT YOUR THESIS HERE

SORRY, YOUR MARGINS ARE 0.07" WIDER THAN UNIVERSITY SPECIFICATIONS.
COME BACK TOMORROW.

IS THIS IT? ARE WE BREAKING UP?
MAYBE FOR NOW IT'S FOR THE BEST.

I'M SORRY.
ME TOO.
JORGE CHAM © 2007

WHEN'S YOUR FLIGHT OUT AGAIN?
NEXT WEEK.
AWKWARD.

OK, VERY GOOD. CONGRATULATIONS.
YOU'LL GET YOUR DIPLOMA IN THE MAIL.
THAT'S IT?
NEXT!

JORGE CHAM © 2007

OKAY...
NOW WHAT?

Original sketch for the comic in page 74.

THE 2005-2006
SPEAKING TOUR
SINCE IT WAS DIFFICULT TO DRAW REGULAR COMIC STRIPS WHILE ON TOUR, HE INSTEAD POSTED STORIES OF LIFE ON THE ROAD FROM A TRAVEL LOG HE KEPT IN HIS NOTEBOOK. MANY READERS SAW THIS AS A FUN CHANGE OF PACE FOR THE COMIC AND AN INTERESTING OPPORTUNITY TO SEE WHAT LIFE IS LIKE IN OTHER GRADUATE SCHOOLS. OTHERS THOUGHT IT WAS BORING AND SELF-INDULGENT.
IN ANY CASE, HERE THEY ARE REPRINTED IN THEIR ENTIRETY.
GRAD SCHOOL
LIFE
HAPPINESS
$
DURING THE 2005-2006 ACADEMIC YEAR, JORGE CHAM WAS INVITED TO SPEAK AT 57 UNIVERSITIES IN THE U.S. AND CANADA.
U. Alberta
U. Calgary
U. Washington
U. California Davis
UC Berkeley
Stanford U.
U. Southern California
UCLA
Scripps Inst.
UC San Diego
U. Colorado
U. Utah
College
U. New Mexico
UT Austin
Texas A&M
Virginia Tech
UT Med. Branch
Rice U.
RPI
Dartmouth
Yale U.
Harvard
U. New Hampshire
Clark U.
MIT
Boston U.
U. Mass Boston
Brown U.
U. Rhode Island
Princeton U.
U. Delaware
U. Penn/Drexel U.
Johns Hopkins U.
U. Maryland
College of William and Mary
CMU
U. Virginia
Virginia Commonwealth
NC State
U. Georgia
Georgia Tech

A PHD FIELD JOURNAL

CU-BOULDER

© JORGE CHAM

A presenter's worst nightmare: my laptop wouldn't project on the screen

Fortunately, audience-member Wendy saves the day.

Audience member Wasim was frowning throughout the talk

why is that guy so upset?

blah blah

"I was just squinting b/c I couldn't see the screen," he later explained.

Signed books for the "Hotchick Lab"

An actual All-female Physics Lab.

Was assisted in book sales by Arwen...

Whose dad named her after the Lord of the Rings character

THE SACNAS (SOCIETY FOR ADVANCEMENT OF CHICANO AND NATIVE AMERICANS IN SCIENCE) NATIONAL CONFERENCE

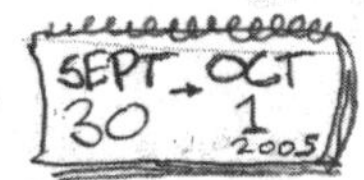

PhD fan Ana Luisa's advisor once got injured playing racquetball with a student.

A case of "no-life imitates art"?

The conference shared the convention center with THE GREAT AMERICAN BEER FESTIVAL

It wasn't hard to tell the attendees apart.

Signed a book that grad student Edgardo swears he'll give to his dept. head, Jim Watson

(Watson is the Nobel laureate who co-discovered the structure of DNA)

Post-doc boothmate Shelly (a Tajel look-alike, she even went to Berkeley undergrad) ...

recounts horror stories of the psycho advisor she endured for 5 years. 5 years!!

CRAZY DAY: pulled an all-nighter, sprinted to airport, rushed to give a research seminar, met with faculty, did a TV interview for a local station, performed PhD talk, signed books, went to bar with grad students, then got up at 5 am to catch next flight out. (Phew!)

does grad school make you dumber? yes.

Was also invited for drinks at a professor's gorgeous Bauhaus-designed house overlooking the mountains:

He paid less for it than what I paid for my 2 bedroom condo in L.A.

Grad student Tamara, who models how stars flow around black holes,

ooh...

explains to me that the sun is made up of layers like an onion.

At the signing, Physics PhD Elizabeth says she is trying to wrap up so she can become a realtor.

I asked her why, and she said: "I rather work with people than particles"

Got a standing ovation from one lone audience member:

After the talk, he was going to the lab: "I sleep better there than I do at home" he explains.

Grad student RAJ asks the unthinkable:

(so, how long did YOUR PhD take?)

WHY, I NEVER!!

In truth, I was afraid I would lose "street cred".

At the ensuing reception, two grads were overheard saying:

They were just there for the FOOD!!

Afterwards, I was taken to

An underground (literally) student-run grad bar where beers are 75¢ and undergrads are given dirty looks.

I wanted to share with the audience funny stories of my time at TECH, but couldn't remember anything

I must have blocked it all out! (though in retrospect, it doesn't seem so bad now compared to grad school)

The auditorium was the same room I took undergrad classes in lifestyle health, real-world engineering economics, and the Eng.-in-Training exam

None of which I actually used in grad school.

Was interviewed for the student newspaper by PRERNA, a freshman from Kuwait

"I was 9 years old when you started grad school", she was kind enough to share.

My parents happened to be in Atlanta and attended the talk

Some PhD fans got the low-down on my childhood.

The lecture was in this crazy M.C. ESCHER maze-like building

Apparently it used to be a structurally unsafe parking deck converted to classrooms based on a design by grad students

The pizza for the event never arrived and the packed lecture hall nearly erupted in a riot

I barely made it out alive!

Event instigator and allround nice guy LEE, who once hiked the appalachian trial,

Is getting paid as faculty at 3X the salary even though he's still years from graduating.

Had dinner with a bunch of Industrial organization psychology grads

According to them, low salary will not make a person quit their job (a fact I'm sure is not lost to university administrators)

VIRGINIA TECH VT in Progressive Blacksburg, VA OCT 28 2005

Football is SO BIG on this campus (the town population doubles on game days) even grads get into it!

(I'm sure it helps that your team is ranked top 3 in the nation)

Funny signing request: a big rubber ball kicked around in lab to relieve stress:

I drew a giant face of prof. smith on it.

Met international student Ameliz, who did her PhD in Physics just so she could stay in the U.S. and take classes to become a professional actress

There's got to be an easier way to get a US visa!

Was invited to an Animal and Poultry Science department Halloween party, but unfortunately, I didn't get the e-mail on time

Ended up at grad hang-out the Watermill, where a fight broke out next to us.

Despite a well-planned event and an amazing spread of free food, attendance was lower than expected.

Still, people seemed to have a good time.

Most of the grads I talked to in this medical sciences campus work on life-saving research

Driving through Virginia, I got a wonderful reminder of how beautiful the Fall colors get here on the east coast

I also got a speeding ticket for going 80 on a 65 mph zone

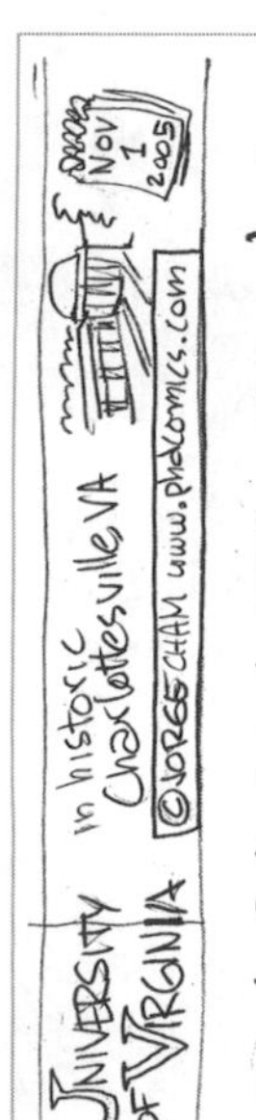

Founded & designed by Thomas Jefferson, the school still observes many of his traditions

Such as no directional signs on ~~campus~~ the "grounds" and calling the faculty "Mr." instead of "Prof."

Event organizer Gavin studies U.S. constitutional Law (even though he's British)

And fights tirelessly for the rights of grad students (e.g. the right to attend football games for free.)

Beers + food at the South St. Brewery with some crazy computer engineering grads:

Johns Hopkins University

in urban Baltimore, MD

©2005 Jorge Cham www.phdcomics.com

Nov 2+4 2005

HOMEWOOD CAMPUS:

Stipends here are so low, many grads with families apply for Welfare (the school president actually encourages it)

Single grads make about $100 too much to qualify for welfare.

At Dizzy Izzie's, Medieval History T.A. Ben recommends dropping 4-letter expletives in class every once in a while...

...to gain the respect of your undergrad students.

MEDICAL SCIENCES CAMPUS:

Tensions run high between the local low-income population and this downtown campus, where armed guards stand at every corner and everyone must wear ID badges

Public health students here get weaned off grad staples like coffee, popcorn and egg salad...

...After learning how bad they really are for you.

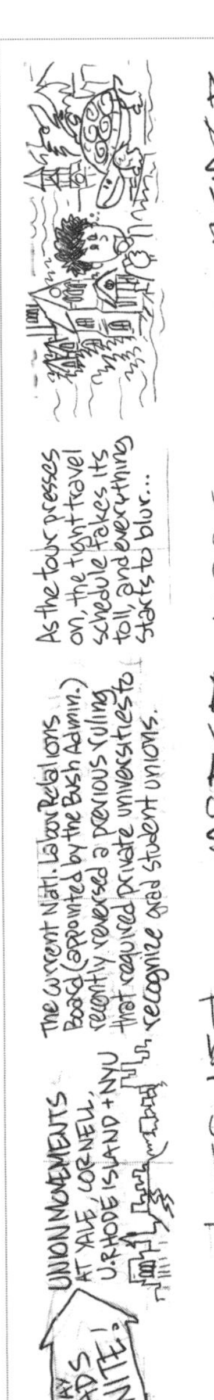

...and Joanne gives "Dissertation Lamaze" classes to her Nursing school students

PUSH!

It's... it's a thesis!

Meanwhile, fans are pulling crazier stunts at the signings (are they just trying to get featured in this journal?)

At Yale, anthropology grad Rob wants a picture taken with his D. Vader mask:

(say "sith"!)

At Drexel, I get handed a ramen package wrapped flower bouquet

thank you

thank you

AT YALE, university administrators leaned on ANGELA's advisor to discourage her efforts to start a sciences union

they can't intimidate me!

Tho she is passionate about the right to unionize, the difficulties and apathy of her fellow students make her start to lose hope.

At NYU, hundreds of grads (and some faculty) march around Washington square on the first day of a campus wide STRIKE

In response, the administration issues veiled threats and propaganda emails portraying grads as spoiled and irresponsible to the poor suffering undergrads.

In Cornell, the union issue was put to a popular vote, and was rejected 2:1 by grad students

Auto workers + grad students in the same union doesn't make sense.

Many saw the movement as sketchy and manipulative and thought the anti-union group (~~sponsored by campus conservatives~~) made more sense.

At the Univ. of Rhode Island, the union movement enjoyed wide Faculty support, and were incorporated in the existing Faculty Union.

With OUR diet...

We NEED dental insurance!

At the heart of the issue is whether grads are STUDENTS or EMPLOYEES who have the right to bargain collectively.

teach my class.

It's good for you.

Support for unions seems split along humanities/social science grads and engineering/sciences grads (who earn more money)

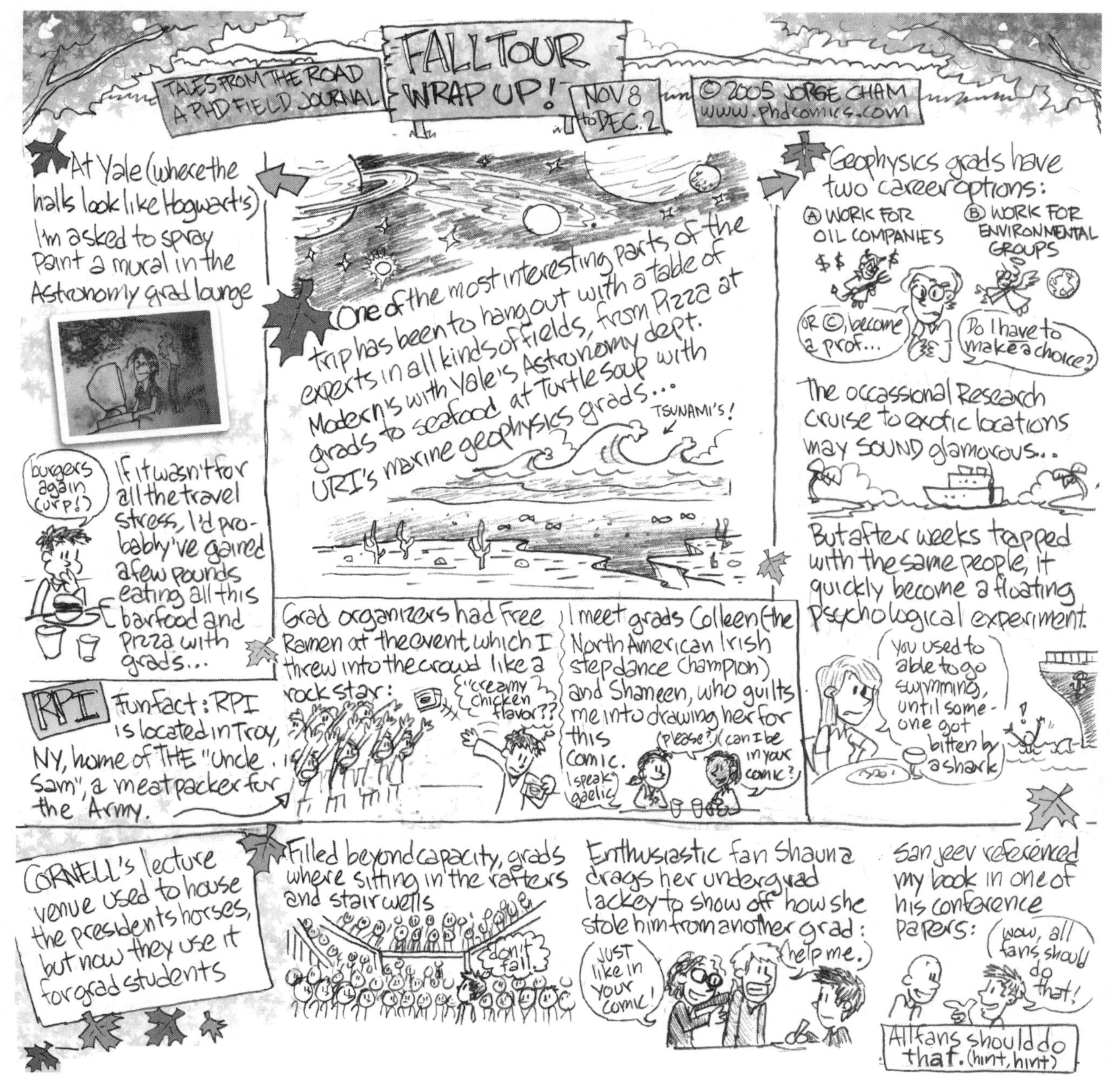
TALES FROM THE ROAD
A PHD FIELD JOURNAL
FALL TOUR WRAP UP!
NOV 8 to DEC. 2
© 2005 JORGE CHAM
www.phdcomics.com
At Yale (where the halls look like Hogwart's) I'm asked to spray paint a mural in the Astronomy grad lounge
burgers again (urp!)
If it wasn't for all the travel stress, I'd probably've gained a few pounds eating all this barfood and pizza with grads...
One of the most interesting parts of the trip has been to hangout with a table of experts in all kinds of fields, from Pizza at Modern's with Yale's Astronomy dept. grads to seafood at Turtle Soup with URI's marine geophysics grads...
TSUNAMI'S!
Geophysics grads have two career options:
Ⓐ WORK FOR OIL COMPANIES
$ $
Ⓑ WORK FOR ENVIRONMENTAL GROUPS
OR ©, become a prof...
Do I have to make a choice?
The occassional Research cruise to exotic locations may SOUND glamorous...
But after weeks trapped with the same people, it quickly become a floating psychological experiment.
You used to able to go swimming, until someone got bitten by a shark
RPI
Fun Fact: RPI is located in Troy, NY, home of THE "Uncle Sam", a meatpacker for the Army.
Grad organizers had Free Ramen at the event, which I threw into the crowd like a rock star:
"creamy chicken flavor??
I meet grads Colleen (the North American Irish stepdance champion) and Shaneen, who guilts me into drawing her for this comic.
(please?)
(can I be in your comic?
I speak gaelic
CORNELL's lecture venue used to house the presidents horses, but now they use it for grad students
Filled beyond capacity, grads where sitting in the rafters and stairwells
don't fall.
Enthusiastic fan Shauna drags her undergrad lackey to show off how she stole him from another grad:
JUST like in your comic!
help me.
San Jeev referenced my book in one of his conference papers:
wow, all fans should do that!
All fans should do that. (hint, hint)

PRINCETON

My trusty 5-yr-old laptop finally gives up and dies. It held up almost to the end of the tour.

No more!

goodbye old friend.

I'm taken to the "De-basement" another underground grad-run Bar/nightclub, complete with a DJ and a bartender everyone says looks like Cecilia

It was so packed and hip, my dorky self felt out of place.

U. NEW MEXICO

I'm on campus for the annual tradition of lighting thousands of candle-filled paper bags everywhere

I met the university President, who almost walked off with a fan's PHD book that was handed to him to explain what my lecture was about.

thank you.

It's MINE!

A brief struggle ensued to explain to the prez the book WASN'T a gift.

TOUR STATS

OF SCHOOLS ON FALL TOUR: 19

TOTAL # OF LECTURE ATTENDEES: 2700

TOTAL # OF BOOKS SIGNED: 1000

my hand

MILES DRIVEN: 2600 miles

OF TIMES I WAS ASKED HOW LONG I WAS IN GRAD SCHOOL: PRICELESS

NOW LEAVING 2005

MORE SCHOOLS NEXT YEAR!

see you then...

UNIVERSITY OF WASHINGTON, JAN. 19, 2006

The event was a rare co-sponsorship between the EE and CS departments, who are usually at odds over space and facilities...

for one night, though, there was peace.

Before the talk, I am handed a written proposal on why I should include in this comic a snack shop that a few grads run from their office in the fourth floor.

later, i get a tour (but no free snacks)

Grad student Sandra tells me at the signing:

I started to tear up when she said that!

Later, at the Big Time Brewery, a bunch of grads trade geeky "An engineer, a mathematician and a physicist walk into a bar..." jokes for hours:

(they were shocked to discover I don't actually drink beer, even though people are always taking me to bars)

UNIV. CALIFORNIA, DAVIS
JAN. 23, 2006

The place has its roots as an agriculture school (you can get class credit for butchering and horseback riding, among other things)

The campus Wi-Fi system is called the "MOObile Network")

The talk is attended by Emil, director of grad counseling services...

who promptly started napping in the middle of my talk.

Exiting grad student Chris says he's applied to faculty positions in 109 schools, "just in case"

SCRIPPS RESEARCH INSTITUTE AND UNIV. CALIFORNIA SAN DIEGO, FEB. 8, 2006

After a week in Canada, I am amazed by the sunny weather and gorgeous beaches these schools are next to.

and yet, the grad students don't seem any less miserable here...

UNIV. CALIFORNIA LOS ANGELES, FEB. 23, 2006

The talk was organized as a Grad Bar Happy Hour (free booze!), so it was a well-liquored audience.

everything i said was HILARIOUS to them.

I start to feel my age when the campus undergrad cartoonist asks for my advice.

A couple of grads give me a hard time for calling Anthropology a Humanities...

I meet super-giddy Rebecca, who claims to be my #1 UCLA fan...

...and soft-spoken Elaine, who was so stressed out by grad school at some point, she had seizures in the lab.

UNIV. SOUTHERN CALIFORNIA, FEB. 22, 2006

Niyati's advisor became nice to her after she developed carpel tunnel syndrome in her wrists

(little does he know, she got it from playing Sudoku online so much!)

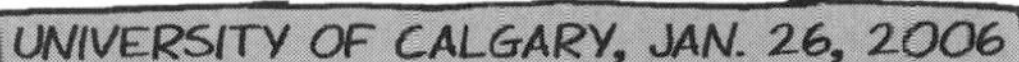

Students here were trying to explain the socio-economic role Alberta Province plays within Canada's culture. Finally, they said:

Walking around, I'm told how lucky I am it's such a beautiful day

Towards the end of each signing, I let people request a character sketch. Usually, it's a good mix, but here, every single person requests Mike.

UNIVERSITY OF ALBERTA, JAN. 27, 2006

The tour schedule is running me ragged: I only slept two hours the night before, so before my talk I take a nap in one of the student center couches.

what! where?? i'm in Canada!?

An hour later, I wake up completely disoriented with no idea where I am!

Event organizer Vince, reveals his secret passion:

cancer diagnostics researcher by day. .

The talk runs late, and we're ushered out of the lecture hall by a miffed prof. and surly undergrads

KANSAS STATE UNIVERSITY, FEB. 10, 2006

Before the talk, I'm given a tour of the university's Konza ecological reserve, where I bond with some of the bison that roam the prairie

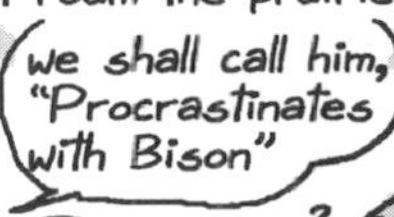

I also bond with a few grad students who roam the campus:

Bala tells me she lives in her advisor's basement

does he throw food down to you?

Kathy studies prairie chicken mating behavior

"I was hoping to gain insight on how men think," she says.

Architecture PhD Matt lives in the house he built for his research

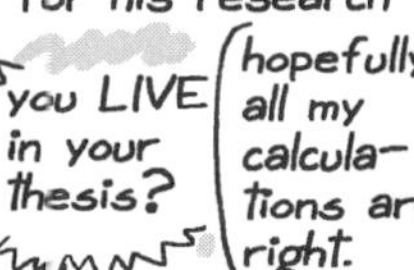

Twin sisters Celina and Marina are both getting their PhD in Geology (how cute!)

Celina saves her thesis on the USB drive she carries around her neck all the time.

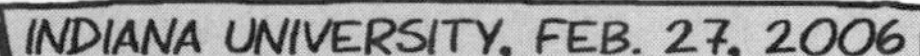

Driving in, I see a Billboard that says:

At the signing, someone compliments me how well i emulate nameless guy's posture.

Over dinner, grad gov. president Paul reveals he was a child chess prodigy:

one of nation's top players by the 8th grade

can play 10 people at the same time

ranked in the World Chess Federation

Psych grad Taylor tells me he's never short of subjects for his experiments:

All Intro to Psychology undergrads are required to participate in at least three experiments.

PURDUE UNIVERSITY, FEB. 28, 2006

I'm given a tour of the mother of all student-run snack shops: the Eta Kappa Nu basement coffee shop:

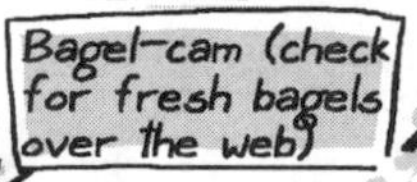

i came to grad school to run a coffee shop?

28,000 bottles of coke and 15,000 cups of coffee sold per year

Shop is located in the same room the Vacuum Tube was invented!

At the signing, ex-grad student Amy describes how she felt when she finally defended her thesis:

I drive west from Indiana for hours through corn fields as far as the eye can see, and into...

UNIV. ILLINOIS, URBANA-CHAMPAIGN, MAR. 1, 2006

At the lecture, I could tell the over-flowed crowd was getting restless for the donuts that were reserved for the signing

Waiting in line, assistant prof. Stephen maintained productivity doing one-handed standing typing on his laptop:

Big surprise: at the lecture were two people I went to High School with (in Panama). Here? In the middle of ~~nowhere~~ Illinois!

Went for pizza with CS students afterwards and some of them were from my alma mater, Georgia Tech!
what year were you there? Maybe I knew you.
we started freshman year in 1999.
never mind.
(I graduated in 1997)
Our waitress was a student in one of the grads' TA section.
hey, you're my TA! bastard.
uh, really?
please don't spit on our food.
NORTHWESTERN UNIVERSITY, MAR. 2, 2006
Over tapas, my friend Malcolm (an assistant prof here) tells me he's still figuring out how to motivate his students.
yeah, threats don't seem to work.
mmm, spanish bar food!
The trick, he says, is to tap into what makes them get out of bed each morning.
Talking to someone who loooves being a professor so much makes me wonder:
...do i love it?
UNIV. CHICAGO, MAR. 3, 2006
Before the talk, event organizer Lieve gives me an exclusive secret tour of the Rockefeller Carillon, the huge bell tower in the middle of campus (being a minor celebrity has its perks)
second largest musical instrument in the world (100 tons, 72 bells)
Amazing view of Chicago
dark narrow catwalks and spiral staircases (like Hunchback of NotreDame!)
I'm treated to a duet performance, which is heard all throughout campus.
can you play the Imperial March?
Sometimes fans travel great distances to come to my talks, but Washington U. grad Audra is the new record holder:
i drove 5 hours to hear you speak
thank you.
At happy hour, I try to eat a slice of Chicago style pizza.
is there bread in there?
defibrillator anyone?
UNIV. NEW HAMPSHIRE, FEBRUARY 15, 2006
The talk was well attended due in large part to a huge gaggle of sorority girls that sat in the back rows.
that's... unusual.
Someone informs me it's pledge week, so I'm guessing a senior sister PhD fan probably forced them all to come.
HAHAHA!
oh. my. god. this is, like, so dorky.
I could tell who she was: she was the only one laughing.
Afterwards, older grad student Bob tells me he's made a bet with his teenage daughter that he'll graduate before she finishes high school.
They call me "Dr. Dad"
the house always wins.

DARTMOUTH ~~UNIVERSITY~~ COLLEGE, FEBRUARY 17, 2006

The prof. hosting me was all set to go have lunch with me, when he realized:

actually, i have a meeting with someone more important

eh, i'm used to it.

he double-booked me!

In his absence, his grad students order the most expensive thing on the menu:

Dartmouth proudly maintains the word "College" in its name to assure undergrads that the school is "all about them"

They say prospective freshmen tour guides deny that grad students even exist on campus (or at least, that they teach classes, which they do).

NEW JERSEY INSTITUTE OF TECHNOLOGY, MARCH 6, 2006

I got there early, so i decided to nap in the grad lounge,

ZZZZ

Later, i'm walking around, not realizing i have a huge case of "nap hair"!

Event organizer Peter insists i be escorted to and from the train station.

M.I.T. AND HARVARD, MARCH 8, 2006

At M.I.T, I'm complimented how much more polished the talk is compared to last year...

This came in handy later that afternoon, when my body crashes from exhaustion in the middle of my talk at Harvard.

blacking out ... must not ... faint...

BLAH BLAH BLAH...

Somehow, auto-pilot kicked in and the words kept coming out of my mouth.

At the time the talk was set to start, the room was nearly empty, which stressed me out.

exactly ten minutes late, the room suddenly fills to capacity.

While the talk was still going on, a pack of physics grads attempted to bluff their way into the free food.

Staff members managed to keep them at bay.

Afterwards, conversation over drinks with Harvard grads at the Enormous Room (Cambridge's most "tragically hip" lounge) reaches extreme highs and lows:

From the latest research in cloud formation...

...to arguing over appropriate booty size and shaking.

U. MASS-BOSTON, MARCH 9, 2006

Organizers went the extra mile and got a liquor license (and required cop) for the event.

so, what the talk about?

i didn't do it! Sir!

American Studies grad Amanda has a cool thesis topic:

The Dave Matthews Band grassroots phenomenon

BOSTON UNIVERSITY, MARCH 14,

I sign books for Adam and Eva, who started dating in grad school.

not exactly paradise, is it?

Afterwards, members of the BU Rat Sex Research Group take me out to a bar

my project is to make dildos for rats.

BROWN UNIVERSITY, MARCH 15, 2006

Carting boxes of PHD books like a traveling salesman, I'm suddenly aware how many old university buildings are not made to be ADA (Am. Disabilities Act) compliant

great.

At the signing, some girl randomly hands me her phone

uh, hello?

WHO IS THIS? WHY ARE YOU TALKING TO MY GIRL??

this is the PhD comics guy.

oh, hey dude, I love your comics!

CLARK UNIVERSITY, MARCH 16, 2006

I sign a poster for Shelly, who said when her now-boyfriend saw it, he recognized it

hey, PHD comics!

That's when I knew he was a keeper.

That's right, fellas, reading PHD comics can help you score with the ladies!

Jason tells me horror stories of his old advisor, who would rub it in by saying,

whose name is it on the door?

Before he quit, Jason wrote HIS name in the top edge of the prof.'s name plate, where nobody would see it.

I land in the upper Michigan Peninsula (the "UP") in the dead of Winter:

The atmosphere of snow and abandoned copper mine towns feels just like fellow roboticist Karl Iagnemma describes in his short stories (Google his name and buy his book)...

Though later at MIT he confesses:

actually, i've never been there.

what imagination!

grads treat me to lunch at the conveniently named local bar, "The Library":

can't talk now, mom, i'm at the library!

is that music?

THE MAYO CLINIC

March 21, 2006

on the ride from the airport, i do the head bob from tour tiredness (embarrasing!)

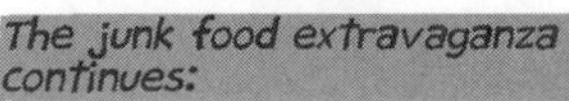

The junk food extravaganza continues:

pizza lunch with a round table of grads:

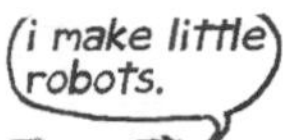

Burgers at Newt's for dinner:

Here at the clinic, the class divide between the med school and the graduate school is no secret...

the med student lounge:

the grad student lounge:

Grad student stories:

Melissa plants "knock-knock" jokes in her paper drafts to see if her advisor actually reads them.

Steve, a.k.a. "The Fungus Guy", is famous for showing cell porn movies in his quals presentation:

Meanwhile, Kristin's quals were marked by one of her profs **hitting on her Mom:**

U. OF IOWA

March 23, 2006

David, my airport ride, explains what his research in Philosophy consists of:

he tells me there are no presentations at Philosophy conferences

people just get up and read their papers!

At the signing, Jessica tells me she thought grad school stress was giving her stomach pains...

...and econ grad James tells me his research is on the financial politics of "World of Warcraft", an online fantasy game (over 7 million players!)

At around this time, I published a field journal comic saying I don't drink beer.

(see 3/21/06 comic)

Since then, schools I've visited assume i have a moral stance against alcohol, and instead of bars, they take me to nice restaurants...

In fact, I'm just more of a cocktails/wine guy, but I don't mind the nice food!

i stay up 'til 2am drawing a comic, just in time to hear the undergrads stumble out of the local bars and clubs:

On the 5am ride back to the airport, sleep researcher Adele tells me:

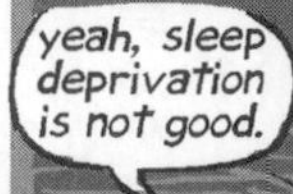

MORE...
TRUE TALES from the Road
Super TEXAS-sized Spectacular!
YEE-HAW!
A PhD FIELD Journal
WWW.PHDCOMICS.COM
COPYRIGHT JORGE CHAM
TEXAS A&M
March 27, 2006
TEXAS A AND M UTAUSTIN AND UTMEDICALBRANCH
AFter criss-crossing the country in coach, I get a taste of Texas hospitality with a first-class flight to College Station...
First time?
Yee-haw!
How the other half flies:
warm towels
free cocktails
gourmet food
upscale version of in-flight magazine
YACHTS
VILLAS
GOLF!
My second taste of Texas hospitality: I get picked up at the airport...
...in a Horse.
The horses belong to Vet Sciences grad Karla, who raises (and races) them in her "spare" time, and plans to clone them.
what's the point in being a geek if you can't clone your own horse?
Airport security didn't think it was that funny, and followed us all the way to the freeway entrance.
ride like the wind!
go!
munch

More hospitality: A Texas-sized gift basket in my hotel room. Contents:

3 t-shirts, cotton candy, cheese, sausage, crackers, stuffed animal, jacket, hat, mug, 2 Aggie books, jelly-beans, calculator, notepads, 3 toys, 3 pens, lint remover, cinna-rolls, 4 bottles of water, 2 juices, mints, stickers and a wig.

WELCOME DR. CHAM!

I'm given a tour of campus and all the crazy Aggie traditions (or at least, the "grad student" tour of campus):

Like at several schools now, I'm told the talk organizers had to hold meetings to discuss how my name is pronounced.

Aggie grads I met:

Joe has been in grad school so long, his two kids have no concept of a "job"

I meet a ringer for one of the PHD charac-ters:

(she also has black belts in 3 martial arts)

I'm short, geeky, dark haired, wear red and my name IS Cecilia!

At dinner, I meet Olivier, a french grad student that actually wants to move to Texas.

i love ze americans!

a french americo-phile??

U.T. AUSTIN
March 28, 2006

WOOT

I almost get lynched making my way through the crowd that had formed outside the locked lecture hall.

by far the rowdiest crowd of all the schools i've been to (and no booze!), the talk took a good 20 extra minutes to get through...

...except for grad student Beth, who could feel her advisor's eyes burning in the back of her head a few rows back...

No signing, but afterwards, Fabio brings his Sugar Mama to thank me:
you saved our marriage.
i thought i'd married a freak, but now i know i'm not the only one!
Later, at a rooftop bar on Weird Austin's 6th St., I hear crazy stories from a group I assumed was composed of shy normal people.
weekly drinking parties!
hook-ups with prospective grad students!
taking clothes off at department BBQ's!
You're Astronomers!?
U.T. MED. BRANCH AT GALVESTON
March 30, 2006
I finagle my way to a tour of the med school's historic and airy dissection lab and the anatomical theatre (now used only to dissect quals presentations)
i'll stick to being a fake doctor, thank you.
I hear stories of when Hurricane Rita was headed straight for Galveston...
"we had to pack what we could..."
Galveston
"put down all animal subjects..."
"none of us expected our labs to be there when we came back..."
Biology grad Tracy confesses that she was secretely hoping the hurricane would wipe out her lab so she'd have an excuse for not having any data.
I saw it as a sign that I was not happy in grad school.
ya think?
COLL. OF WILLIAM AND MARY
March 24, 2006
My airport ride is on "Cecilia", the red car PHD fan Meghan named after the character:
uh...
THE TYPICAL GRAD STUDENT CAR:
equipment for the 10 different sports tried over the years
accumulated crap you're not sure you want to throw away.
overdue library books
at least 10 yrs old
junk food containers
hold on, let me move some stuff.
I get the drive-by tour of Colonial Williamsburg, "Where America Began," allowing me to join the millions of Americans who can say:
i've been here on a school trip!

At the legendary bitter rival school of my alma mater, I take a stand for good ol' Georgia Tech:

Grad student Kenton's comments on my talk trigger some tough questions:

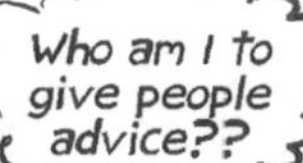

UNIV. OF MICHIGAN
April 3, 2006

At the book signing, a gaggle of female Physics grads shuffles over to my table:

A post-doc tells me he barely heard about the talk tonight because post-docs aren't on any of the announcement lists.

Grad student Ray shows me his book, which is full of sticky bookmarks:

CARNEGIE MELLON U.
April 1, 2006

Jon shows me the ratty t-shirt his advisor offered to buy off him for $10 so he'd stop wearing it in front of sponsors.

Raja thinks CS grad students should wear lab coats to work every day.

William shows me the PERL code he typed in the shape of a heart to propose to his girlfriend.

The geek fest continued the next day with a tour of the Robotics Institute:

At the signing, Bookstore manager Tom tells me I sold more books than sex-advisor "Dr. Ruth" did at her signing the previous week.

PENN STATE UNIV.
April 7, 2006

The talk is sponsored by the Nutrition Department Graduate Student Association, which I see as an opportunity to finally ask the question:

UNIV. MARYLAND BALTIMORE COUNTY
April 28, 2006

I'm introduced to the audience by the University President himself, who worked the crowd by taking cheap shots at me:

HARVEY MUDD COLLEGE
May 3, 2006

The undergrads here seem so convinced their tough curriculum prepares them for the agony of grad school, none of them take my warning seriously...

Well, at least I tried...

UNIV. DELAWARE
April 27, 2006

Grad students Nadya and Gina literally empty their pockets and pool all their money to buy a single PHD book:

During the free food event, graduate provost Mary Martin keeps watch over who is eating the food:

ARE YOU A GRAD STUDENT?

Quick! Answer this question:

You just ran out of money, who do you go to?

uh, my parents?

UNDERGRAD

THIS WEEK: "Coming Full Circle"
Back to where it all began: U.C. Berkeley and Stanford U.

May 4, 2006

To the packed auditorium, I make a shocking revelation:

Imagine a world where I DIDN'T go to Stanford... a World WITHOUT PHD Comics!!

Grad students actually doing work.

I have coffee that afternoon with Wendy Northcut, who started the Darwin Awards to honor those who voluntarily take themselves out of the gene pool.

STANFORD! May 5, 2006

The talk is held in a part of campus I didn't even know existed in my 6 years there.

The talk was organized by WEE (Women in Electrical Engineering):

All 5 of them.

In the audience:

The pressure would have surely cracked a novice. After giving the talk 60 times in 60 cities, though, auto-pilot saved the day.

FREQUENTLY ASKED TOUR QUESTIONS!

① Do you have like a million frequent flyer miles now?

② So, what do you do now? What's your job?

③ Having visited all these schools, what insights have you gained about the state of graduate education in this country? Are grad students the same everywhere?

Afterword by... you.

A random selection of comments submitted to the PHD website during the making of this book

"Hi Jorge. I was wondering, what happens with all those procrastination skills when you become a professor? How do professors procrastinate? Can you enlight me on this matter with one of your strips?"
-Andres, Aerospace Eng - Tohoku University, Japan

"A female student ahead on me in line at a free food event loading her plate with burgers was overheard saying: 'I used to be a vegetarian, then I came to grad school and became an opportunist'"
-CeCe, Soil Microbiology, Washington State University

"Hi Jorge. My name is Imam from Indonesia. I love your comics. I'm pretty shocked that the situation my country is similar with the situation depicted in your comic. I've always thought that the situation abroad is much better. Especially in a famous university like Stanford U. I guess that gives me hope."
-Imam, Human Resources Management, University of Indonesia

"Last night, for a 'crazy night off,' I decided to read PhD comics from the beginning. It's Saturday at noon now, and I start to wonder what the heck I'm doing. How will I ever have the discipline to finish my dissertation when I'm wasting hours and hours of weekend quality work time reading comics rather than grading papers or reading about subjectivity in the 18th C. novel or the labor implications of sex work? Also, I'm really hungry for Ramen now."
-Sofia, English, Rice University

"I was wondering if Cecilia would consider going out with a mysterious and charming Pakistan man (the true tall dark and handsome stuff). I've passed quals!"
-Waqas, Electrical Engineering, Stanford U.

"Here's an advisor story for you: during the hurricanes last year, my advisor 'let' me stay in her damaged house and take care of her dogs when my apartment was destroyed, while she and her family stayed in her parents' winter home. The dogs were impossible, the power didn't work and there was no safe drinking water, but at least I got the use of her personal library."
-Vanessa, English, Florida State University

"It's been only a few days but I'm already a devoted fan! My brother's a Ph.D. candidate in the U.S. and your comic explains why he was in such a terrible shape when he last came home. From now on, I'll try to be a more understanding sister."
-Young, English-Korean Translation, Ewha Women's University, Korea

"I love the advisor jokes! They're my favorite. Need more advisor jokes!"
-Angele, Art History, U. of Montreal

"I hope someone out there is listening to what we grad students have to endure!"
-Sheba, Genetics grad student

“Dear Jorge, I am one of 'the Profs' and I love your comic strip! You do such a magnificent job of capturing so many of the foibles of the system and the people. At least some of us can appreciate the view from both sides of it enough to get a good laugh. My favorite funny prof-student moment from my own lab is this scene from a couple of years ago: I had reached the point of being completely barricaded in front of my computer doing grants and papers, and decided to go back into the lab to do an experiment, the first one in several years. I picked out a bench, picked up a pipettor, and reached for a bottle with a sterile buffer solution in it. From all sides, lab people converged on me, saying "can we help you?" in tones of alarm, and one of them even reached out to take the pipettor away as if I were a two year old with scissors.

I realized that the latest batch of students had no concept of me at a lab bench. Even though I had done a thesis, a postdoc, early research of my own until I had enough funds to fill out a lab, none of them could picture me 30 years ago, working 80 hour weeks in cold rooms surrounded by mile-high stacks of agar plates and DNA stocks as I carried out sequencing reactions with carcinogens and rocket fuel. Thanks for doing these comics. I gave a couple of your books to another prof for her birthday recently and she reacted like I did, that she had hardly seen anything so funny in years!”
-Jane, Genomics, University of Michigan

“Dear Phd, I am a Phd candidate from Turkey who studies in Japan. I like reading your comic strips. Seeing all these kind of losers makes me feel much better.”
-Barkan, Robotics, Yokohama National U., Japan

“Great to see more Tajel featured in the comic! Power to the people... even if they are an amorphous historically contingent socially constructed category.”
-Mike, Sociology of Science, U. of Nottingham UK

“Hi Jorge. I suffer from a terrible human being who happens to be my "advisor". I was wondering if you can make my experiences into a comic. I was thinking maybe you can humorize it to alleviate my resentment.”
-Anonymous

Your comics are great but I have to know, is Cecilia's blog really written by Cecilia? Is she really real? I'm so confused!
-Maxine, Latin Poetry, U. of Sydney

“I just wanted to say that there are days that your comic strips are the only thing that makes me smile and see myself under a sympathetic light.”
-Sotiria, European Studies, LSE

“How about a comic about the chemistry Prof who is having a seriously bad day because he didn't win the Nobel prize and then takes it out on his grad students by cussing at them?”
-Amy, anonymous grad student

“I'm currently in Antarctica doing some fieldwork. Whenever I have a flat moment I read your comics and feel better. In those moments of self doubt and the stomach wrenching feeling that there is no meaning in your life it is comforting to know that it is just part of the experience and that you are not the only one feeling this way....sigh.”
-Camilla, Atmospheric Physics, U. of Tasmania, Australia

“I defend my dissertation in one hour and I'm reading PhD for another 59 minutes!”
-Nick, Physical Chemistry, The U. of Memphis

“Wow, this is a truly wonderful comic. I just started grad school and reading your comic made me feel connected to something bigger. :)”
-Becky, Environmental and Energy Policy, U. of Delaware

"I wanted to thank you for making Tajel a not-so-granola humanities major. It would have been really easy to just leave her as the typical angry-vegan-hardcore-protesting-armpit-hair radical variety we all sort of get labeled as. I deal with enough of those on a daily basis!"
-Jen, Sociology, Concordia U.

"Here's an idea for a strip: I have 3 friends who have started to resemble their profs during the past 2 years, like pets who look like their owners. I think that means it's time to graduate."
-Lauren, Biology Education, Purdue U.

"The other day I was in the restroom, combing my hair, when a fellow grad student rushed in and madly began grabbing paper towels from the dispenser. Flip, flip, flip went the lever as they came out. "Is everything OK?," I asked. "Fine, just fine," came the strained answer. Flip, flip, flip. I followed her to her office, and found her on the floor, trying to sop up a pot of spilled coffee. But I gasped as I saw what she was wiping off--her office mate's research notes for her thesis!"
-Hope, Sociology, U. of New Mexico

"Do you think you can change the name that appears when you minimize the page (i.e. 'Piled Higher and Deeper') to something more studious-looking like 'Current topics in DNA analysis' or 'Journal Publications- Search engine'? This would greatly help my secret slacking."
-Deanna, Neuroscience, Northwestern U.

"So, I'm crouched on the deck of the Research Vessel Gulf Challenger, my hand attempting to carefully throttle the flow of gas into a sample canister. A torrential rain is falling in sheets, washing across the deck and soaking my notebook. Lightning is reaching down out of the low clouds, lashing the ocean beneath it. *CRACK*BOOM! I fight waves of motion-sickness-induced nausea as I attempt to scrawl notes on my logbook. The captain suddenly heals to port to ride over the crest of a swell, the boat wallows, and I have to close my eyes and concentrate very hard to save my lunch. It was then that I started to question my grip on reality: 'Gee,' I thought, 'If we get a paper out of this, my name had better be on it.'"
-Karl, Chemistry, U. of New Hampshire

"Hey. In our lab we carefully monitor the recipient list of the professor's emails to watch for changes in the order of recipients which implies, of course, hierarchical changes in the lab. Many feelings have been hurt over this. I think this can be a nice point for a comic strip."
-Assaf, Electrical engineering, Columbia U.

"Dear Jorge, I am a moustached guy. I have been reading your comics for a while. While reflecting on the characters I found that there is none in your archive that has moustache. There are numerous moustached students like me who want to identify ourselves with one of the characters. Could you please take my request and create a moustached character?"
-Pranesh, Linguistics, Indian Inst. of Technology, Bombay (P.S. I can send you my photograph if you wanna take a look at my jet black mousch!)

"Hi Jorge, I had a very strange dream the other night: In my dream, a friend of mine and I somehow got trapped on a ship. We really didn't want to be on it and we couldn't get off it or we weren't sure when we could. We even tried jumping ship and swimming to shore (even though I don't know how to swim), but we somehow found ourselves back on the ship. In the end we realized we had to pack ourselves in boxes and ship ourselves off the ship! I think the ship represents our PhD program at MIT. Now if only I could figure out what the box packing thing is in real life!"
-Noreen, Chemical Engineering, MIT

“I’m sitting in the lab on a Friday night, reading about Cecilia web-surfing in the lab on a Friday night. Sigh.”
-Tari, Neuroscience, NYU

“Hi Jorge, we're all huge fans here. Just wanted to know how long before that sandwich in the lab fridge becomes fair game? P.S. When will we see some biology students?”
-Paolo, Biology, Montana

“Your cartoon posted 12/3/2005 contains the often misused ‘tidal wave’ image labeled "tsunamis". That's not what a tsunami would look like. It's more like a rapid rise (and drop) in sea level, no tidal wave. And the plural of tsunami is tsunami, like deer. I only say this because I care.”
-Heather, Earth Sci, UCSC

“Across from our Computer Science building here at Stanford, I can see another lab with a girl who, almost on cue at a particular time on certain days, gets up from her desk and starts dancing. Did you observe this phenomena when you were here?”
-Adam, Computer Science, Stanford

“Can I marry Cecilia?”
-Neil Steiner, Electrical Engineering, Virginia Tech

“Universities throughout the world are beginning to respond to the catastrophic devastation that Hurricane Katrina wrought. My home institution is now accepting students whose home institution was affected by the hurricane. Both graduate and undergraduate students can apply for visiting student status and if approved can enroll in courses and other academic programs. More information can be obtained at www.ualberta.ca. All admission decisions will be handled on an individual bases.”
-Tara, Biological Sciences, U. of Alberta

“I'm now in my seventh year of my PhD, and today I decided to create a Mike Slackenerny Fan Club. I don't plan on advertising it because, well, I'm lazy. Now you'll excuse me, I've just been told there's free ice-cream outside.”
-S., computer “stuff” grad student

“For some reason my life is more interesting when it is mimicked in your comics with humor and neat drawings.”
-Steve, Child clinical-psyc, Penn State U.

“Hey, Jorgeeee... I think you are HOT just like your comics ;) are you single?”
-Aileen, Food Science, Michigan State U.

“Hey guys, I love the comic, but after today's strip I'm left irritated once again by your categorization of anthropology into humanities. Why is this? Anthropology is clearly a social science. That's social SCIENCE. C'mon. We're doing real work here, and deserve some respect.”
-Lal, Linguistics, San Francisco State U.

“Love the cartoon about Cecilia ‘dressing to repress’! My twin sister is in Computer Science, and conscientiously does this very same thing. We're constantly emailing cartoons to each other with the heading, ‘This is so you!’
-Nikki, German Studies, U. of Arizona

“Here they put all the new English grad students in the basement. It's terribly dank and depressing, but we write poetry on the walls with Sharpies to keep our spirits up.“
-Karen, English Lit, Florida State U.

“Dear jorge, when can we expect a 3rd PHD comics book? I would love to augment my collection before I graduate (next may?).”
-Katie, Chem Eng, U. Wisconsin-Madison

“Hello, I want to ask you if the strips which appear in color on-line are also colored in the book. Are they?”
-Helder, U. of Porto, Portugal

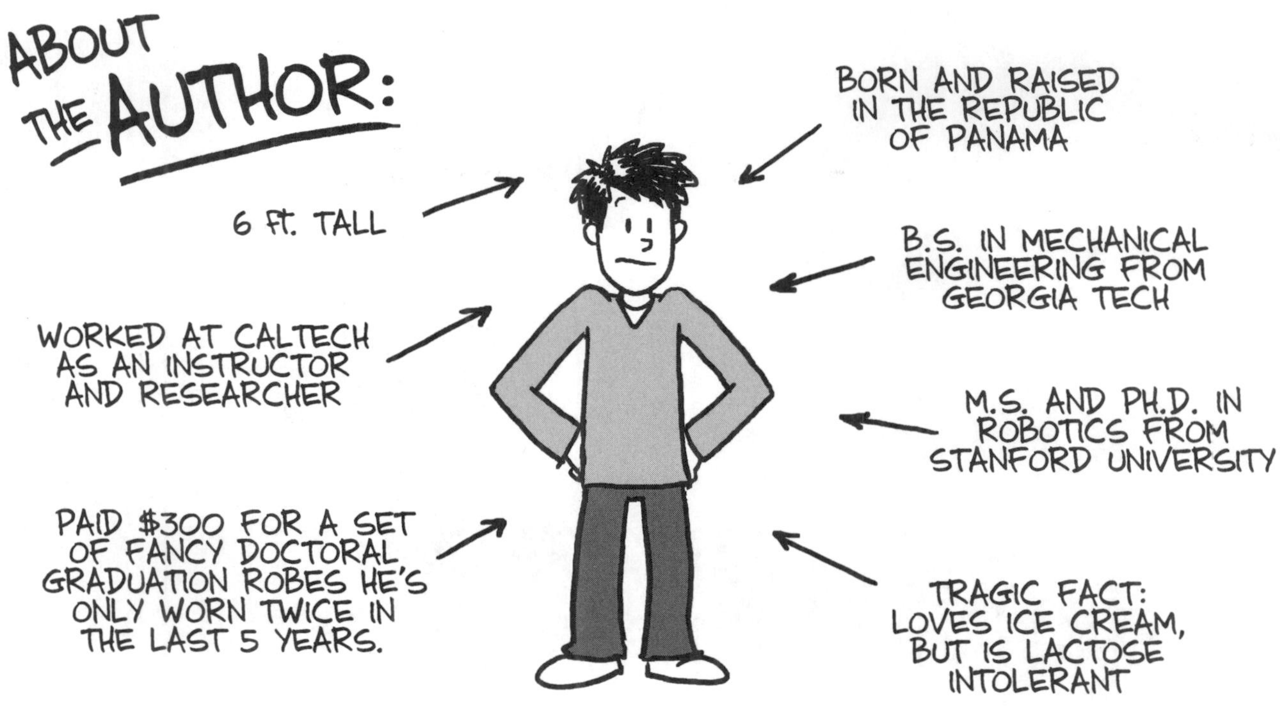

ACKNOWLEDGEMENTS

THIS BOOK IS DEDICATED TO THE READERS OF PHD: THE UNSUNG HEROES WHO BUY THE BOOKS, ORDER THE MUGS AND T-SHIRTS, TELL THEIR FRIENDS ABOUT THE WEBSITE AND WRITE IN WITH COMIC STRIP SUGGESTIONS WHEN THEY "SHOULD" BE DOING RESEARCH INSTEAD. OUR HATS OFF TO YOU, DEAR GRAD STUDENT, WE ARE PROUD TO PROCRASTINATE WITH YOU.

MORE INFO AT: **WWW.PHDCOMICS.COM**